Che in Paona Bazaar

Kishalay Bhattacharjee is a senior journalist who has been with broadcast television for twenty years. Seventeen of those were spent at New Delhi Television (NDTV) where he was a Resident Editor covering conflict in India's north-east as well as in the Maoist corridor.

Bhattacharjee is the recipient of the Ramnath Goenka Award (2006-2007) for his coverage of internally displaced people. He is a Panos Fellow for HIV/AIDS (2007) and an Edward Murrow Fellow in Journalism (2006). His film *Santi, Lucy and Thoibi* was screened at international film festivals in Goa and Barcelona. He was selected as Chair, Internal Security and as a Senior Fellow at the Institute for Defence Studies and Analyses (2011). He is a regular columnist and speaker on conflict and post-conflict situations in India.

Che in Paona Bazaar

Tales of Exile and Belonging from India's North-east

KISHALAY BHATTACHARJEE

MACMILLAN

First published in the Indian subcontinent 2013 by Macmillan
an imprint of Pan Macmillan, a division of Macmillan Publishers Limited

Pan Macmillan, The Smithson, 6 Briset St., Farringdon, London EC1M 5NR
Associated companies throughout the world

www.panmacmillan.com

ISBN 978-93-82616-04-7

Typeset in AGaramond Pro 12 /15.3 by Jojy Philip, New Delhi 110 015

Printed and bound in India by Manipal Technologies limited, Manipal

FSC www.fsc.org MIX Paper | Supporting responsible forestry FSC® C043100

To Bambi, my daughter, with a hope that she grows up to a world which will realize the futility of killing each other

Prologue

GUWAHATI, DECEMBER 2000

An elderly lady with matted hair arranges a few packets of cigarettes and tobacco sachets on a raised wooden platform outside the Guwahati railway station. With a crushed saree draped over her thin body, Buri Ma displays an air of command over her immediate neighbourhood. People walk past her, some stop by to purchase their fix. She is just one amongst the several vendors in a chaotic parking zone of the station. A potbellied policeman claps his hands to air out the tobacco and goes about his business, collecting protection tax. This is a high security zone in a conflict-ridden area where vital locations like railway stations are vulnerable targets and armed groups fighting against the government have often chosen places like this one to plant explosives. It's easy to escape without being noticed.

One day a blast ripped through the railway station. All the vendors were thrown out even though they paid a daily allowance to the police station. In the sanitized parking lot, Buri Ma remained at her kiosk selling cheap cigarettes and an assortment of betel nut and paan. Her cigarettes were special – they were marijuana joints. Intrigued by how she survived the clean-up operation, I chatted up the policeman who had now hiked up his rates from rickshaw-pullers to compensate for the loss he'd incurred since the vendors had departed from the parking lot. He told me how every morning, Buri Ma would catch the local train from the oil township of Narengi to Guwahati railway station. She would arrive by the first shuttle and leave by the last available train. One evening, I travelled with her. She must have been around eighty but her enthusiasm was contagious. Even after the day's work, she was not exhausted and she began to tell me her story.

For a woman so old, Buri Ma has a rather youthful name: Bobby. She doesn't remember who she was born to or how she came to this city. She said she had a different name and how she became Bobby is also rather mysterious, but she never disclosed that part of her story to me. She spoke in Assamese but she said she doesn't belong to any particular community. We crossed a field and took the lane to the namghar or community hall; many years ago, Buri Ma had helped build the place and she proudly showed me around. Every locality in Assam has a community hall where people meet, pray, sing and sometimes perform traditional theatre. The old namghars are generally wooden with some basic sculptures, earthen floor and thatched roofing but the one here has been raised on concrete. It is a large rectangular hall with all four sides open and a high ceiling. Adjacent to the namghar is her own house. On a lower level, a garden leads us to a fairly large house with four rooms. She built the house brick by brick, adding to each wall over a number of years whenever she could afford to spare some money. The rooms extend haphazardly, probably constructed by unskilled artisans but nevertheless it breathes the air of a home.

When she settled down, the land was cheap because it was adjacent to the cremation ground. People generally hesitate to settle down near cremation grounds but the pressure on land has forced many to ignore that and accept what is available. But Buri Ma was quite comfortable with the idea of having a house near a cremation ground. Today the area is a sprawling residential colony of lower-middle class people who aspire to build their own house. Buri Ma is the guardian of the colony. Her selfless engagement in the social life of the colony has endeared her to all.

She sleeps in a room which has little figures and pictures of gods and goddesses from all religions; she says she believes in them all. Outside, in the courtyard, there is a charpoy on which an infant is waiting for her mother's return. A young girl, probably the elder sister, sings a lullaby and feeds the infant a local variety of banana. There is no baby food at home. The infant is the youngest of the seven children Buri Ma has sheltered in this house. Only a week ago, Buri Ma rescued the infant from a garbage dump. Her eldest daughter is married with a child and was visiting Buri Ma. The eldest son works in a bookshop. The others are attending school. All of them were orphans or homeless children – abandoned on roads, railway stations, fields and rescued by Buri Ma. She remembers the first child she brought home was found in an empty railway coupe of the Brahmaputra Mail. She had missed the shuttle home that evening and so she boarded the Mail train. That was twenty-seven years ago.

The children were a happy lot playing with their new kid sister. It is a strange little story of one woman's charity: all the children have been brought up on marijuana sale outside the railway station, with an empathetic police letting her carry on with the business, while saluting her love for abandoned children.

Kolkata, April 2012

Like Buri Ma's story, this is a book made of images, stories of individuals and anecdotes that are part of an ongoing journey in my life. The idea of a book on the socio-political landscape of India's north-east grew out of my journalistic tours and travels into the distant corners of the region and stories that we often do not report because they are just not 'important.'

Everywhere I looked, I was confronted with words and images that represented the north-east in a stereotypical manner: young men and women strumming a guitar or that of a bomb exploding. I have been feeling frustrated about what has not been told or has never been seen simply because it has not been recorded. I strongly feel that there is no single narrative that adequately reflects the complexity of the region and the various ethnicities that inhabit these hills.

My formative years in Shillong were idyllic, only to be cut short by a violent and sustained student movement which coincided with the Assam Agitation of 1979. I remember one evening when the hill facing our house was lit up with a procession of mashals. Our neighbourhood was panic-stricken and I witnessed families packing up their essentials to leave. The indigenous Khasi, Jaintia and Garo tribes had declared war on the non-tribal population. They saw non-tribals as usurpers of employment, educational opportunities and above all, land. The government offices were full of babus, composed of non-tribals, the majority of whom were Bengalis. The tribals felt economically intimidated and threatened. As children we were never exposed to this hostility so the sudden violence shocked us. Initially the indigenous people attacked the Bengalis, then the Nepalis and then all non-tribals came under fire. Massive human rights violations went unreported. A mass exodus went undocumented.

That was Shillong in the 1970s and 1980s and some of the 1990s as well. It was much later when I returned to report from the region that north-east India opened up to me in the least expected way.

Violence is a fact and fear is an emotion that accompanies the daily lives of the people here. But it is also true that post-conflict literature cannot be a testament of collective pain. It is more often than not very personal. Pain has no learning curve and one person's opinion is often different from another's. Sometimes one flips through old albums and pauses at certain photographs, reliving a moment in time. Similarly, I have returned to past journeys and recollected the stories by a roadside tea shop or an army camp or a trek through a World War II supply line.

To steer clear of any incoherence caused by the numerous voices that have spoken to me, a fictional character named Eshei is my storyteller. She embodies the various experiences of growing up, navigating through youth, love and loss in the backdrop of conflict but is also faced with the universal trials of everyday reality.

Eshei tells me how she grew up in an almost-dysfunctional society, how she came to terms with the baggage of an identity based on violence and secessionism. A few other characters, partly fictional, pop up from time to time to narrate their own aspirations. I wanted to show at least a facet of the north-east through their eyes but at the same time, offer an 'outsider's' perspective, up close and personal.

To represent the people as they are, their cuisine, their music, their history or even their biases, I have used the interplay of text and personal correspondence, a mixture of genres which do not follow a linear style. I have tried to show the dispossession and the richness of their stories in fragments, which is evident in the structure of the narrative. It is a personal rendering of a people who are perceived as a single entity, wrongfully identified as a single entity and have been trapped in images that mark them as xenophobic, militant, aggressive, and different from the rest of 'us.'

In my long years of interaction with the people of the north-east, I've felt that they could neither speak the truth of their experience nor even make it heard through the mainstream Indian media. This is an attempt to make the readers interact with real people and not 'imagined communities.' However, this book is limited only to certain areas in the region – Manipur, Guwahati and Shillong. Food is a subject that can weave together the taste of a community and a generation. I travelled through the different cuisine and made the inheritors of these culinary traditions speak for them. Chunks of conversation and correspondence have been reproduced verbatim at places. For some I have changed it slightly to protect identities.

Manipur's music, dance, food and the stories of its people dominate the book. Eshei is there through all the travails and tribulations of a generation caught between the apathy as well as the evolution of a society at crossroads. She brings us the folktales of her land and as the character develops, Eshei grows from being a loner into someone who becomes a part of the events that engulf her state.

There are issues and subjects which would otherwise be avoided for obvious reasons. For example, polygamy in urban Manipur or the genocide by terror groups fighting in the name of identity or even the lighter side of a very emotive students' agitation in Assam.

Conflict makes for interesting stories.

The book almost deliberately skips an important chapter, Nagaland, and cross fades with an abstract image of a short encounter.

On the morning of 19 February 1983, our valve radio set broadcasted a chilling piece of news. The previous day a few thousand immigrant Muslims were hacked to death in Assam. With a blink of an eye, the Nellie massacre placed the north-east on the cover pages of national newspapers and magazines. I witnessed the rise of sub-national assertion in Assam from the sidelines in Shillong, which soon felt the heat of what degenerated into chauvinistic and xenophobic movements.

I've collected anecdotes from those street-fighting years, stories told to me by the soldiers of that rebellion. Some of them are silly but witty as well. Documentation of Assam's and for that matter, the region's contemporary history is grossly inadequate. I felt stories of the people who have witnessed the turbulence and the disillusionment can never be replaced by any alternate fiction or narrative. I have tried to retain much of the flavour of these stories.

Like cuisine, I found that markets in every city tell us about its people and the place. The book explores a number of markets and the ordinary impressions of ordinary people which make up what a place is all about.

Disjointed sequences revisit me – an early twilight in Shillong; my poet friend Robin and I discussing the politics of exile and anti-poetry among other things over bowls of dumplings in a Chinese restaurant and a whiff of ajinomoto. I have plucked those afternoons and made him speak through his poetry of the mooring of a land he left behind.

In the end it is a collaborative effort by many voices about the place and its people, about life itself. The events and descriptions are true, the characters are a combination of the people I have met and interacted with.

I have interviewed a cross-section of people and in each of them I found a courageous willingness to reopen wounds which they had hidden, sometimes even from themselves. In spite of my efforts, I fear that my narrative can only offer a modest glimpse into their lives and I hope that I have been able to capture their real-life experiences, their stories in their voice and often, in their words.

ONE

Che in Paona Bazaar

Touchdown Imphal and the valley embraces you without the tinge of fear that is inspired by the news images of Manipur. But as we drive into the city, groups of armed soldiers patrolling the highway at regular intervals don't instill much confidence. They march on both sides of the road carrying automatic weapons, radio signal equipment and a sense of purpose. A group of men in spotless white dhotis and kurtas ignore the men in fatigues and enter the Krishna temple for morning prayers. It's barely ten in the morning. Children walk to school crossing army barricades. Office-goers get frisked. Nobody complains.

Girls and women speed by on two-wheelers. They're wearing wrap-arounds called 'phaneks' with dupattas woven around their busts and have smeared sandalwood paste on their forehead and the nasal ridge; their appearance is rather conspicous because not one town or city in the region has such a large female following of second generation two-wheelers with the riders in traditional wear. The trend probably started in the 1970s but with the Kinetic Honda model being introduced in the 1990s, almost every woman rides a scooter. The phanek is almost like a sarong and very south-east Asian in its appearance. Married women almost always wear it. But it's only during festivals like Holi when young girls get to wear the phanek, along with the sweet-smelling joiper, the chadar that accompanies the phanek.

The Holi festival that is celebrated in Manipur is a fusion of traditional rituals and Vaishnavite practices. The festival is called Yaoshang – yao means sheep and shang means a hut, a hut for sheep. In this festival, which is an adapted version of Holi, the hut is burnt to celebrate the victory of good over evil. Children go to all the houses in the locality for nakadeng (collecting money as gifts) on the first day of Yaoshang as the shang is burnt only in the evening.

The first time I met Eshei in a village near Imphal, our conversation centred around the phanek. Eshei is not her real name, it's a name she has given herself. 'Eshei' means song in Manipuri. She loved music and though she strummed a guitar with some amount of ease, she didn't display any real talent. She was too impatient to learn and play musical instruments. Eshei's favourite phanek was the Mayek Naiba phanek, the striped ones with embroidered borders that women wear on formal occasions. The first time she wore it was for a cousin's wedding. Her mother tied a string around her waist so that it wouldn't fall off. Wearing the phanek, the fourteen-year-old Eshei felt like a young lady on the brink of womanhood. She realized that feminine curves lent the attire a certain grace that made women so desirable, but she neither had the curves nor the waist to carry this off. Every Meitei (the non-tribal Hindu majority of Manipur who were once a tribal community and ruled over the kingdom of Kangleipak) girl will have a phanek story to share.

Though most married women wear the traditional phanek, young girls were mostly seen in western wear. In 2001, the local fashion changed after a diktat by the militant group Kanglei Yawol Kanna Lup enforced the phanek on all women. It was made compulsory even for school girls. Exactly a decade later, they banned the sari and salwar kameez as well. These bans are not taken very seriously but over the years they have had a visible impact. There are more women and girls wearing the phanek on the streets of Imphal today than one would have seen some years ago.

The day the diktat was passed, one woman defied it by wearing a pair of jeans and walked down the main road in downtown Imphal. I don't think anyone even noticed her. On the same day her niece was wearing a phanek to school. At present, while the school uniform has stuck, urban young women have gone back to wearing fashionable western wear, balanced almost perfectly with traditional wear.

Eshei was in her second year at college when they were asked to wear the phanek to class. Much as she liked wearing it, when they were ordered to do it, she wanted to defy the authorities. Their uniform was a blue phanek with a white top. It was around the same time that the armed outfits decided that all mainstream Hindi culture must also be banned along with Indian apparel and western wear to reinstate the 'lost glory' of Manipur. It was projected as some alien culture out to impose its imperialist designs on the people of Manipur. The otherwise familiar protest placards were not visible against this diktat. The newspapers might have written against it but they failed to have any impact. Nobody was willing to sacrifice one's life defying a dress code which is after all one's own; tradition was conveniently used to up the moral ante of the vigilantes. As always, the 'patriots' of a forgotten and once-betrayed Asiatic sovereign got what they wanted.

The favourite Hindi films were no longer watched since the theatres were shut down. Hindi entertainment channels on satellite television were banned (except the state-run Doordarshan). *Hum Dil De Chuke Sanam* was probably the last time Bollywood visited Manipur on the big screen. By the time Eshei grew up to watch films in theatres, cinema projectors had stopped rolling. She managed to watch both the Hindi and English versions of *Titanic*. Some say the last film to visit the town was *Chori Chori Chupke Chupke*. The name differs with each generation. Maybe that was the end of celluloid in Manipur. Dish television had not invaded the country as yet. But just as Bollywood heroes and heroines disappeared, Korean films and television serials occupied the space.

Doordarshan began airing Korean dramas such as *A Jewel in the Palace* and *Emperor of the Sea*. The popular Korean channel, Arirang, brought home Korean culture, tradition and cuisine. It is around the same time that Korean businesses entered India in a big way with Hyundai cars, LG and Samsung products. But the cultural invasion was felt in Manipur. Significantly, Korean culture was not perceived as 'foreign' by militant leaders. Meiteis are ethno-linguistically from the Tibeto-Burman family. The Koreans are believed to be descendants of several Mongol tribes that migrated from Central Asia; both Meiteis and Koreans are Mongoloids. R K Meghen, the chief of the United National Liberation Front (UNLF), the oldest armed group of the region and Manipur till his arrest in 2010, was working towards a unification of Mongoloid armed groups in India's north-east. They saw similarities in the shared racial background, gestures and communication.

Take for example, the naming practices of each. In both Manipuri and Korean cultures, the family name comes first. Traditional Manipuri names have three parts – the first one is the family name, the second is the actual name of the person, and the third is a suffix, mainly to distinguish the gender of the person. So if the name is Rajkumar Basanta Singh, Rajkumar is the family name, Basanta the personal name, and Singh, the suffix since he is a male. Nicky Chandam's real name should be Chandam Nicky Devi, where Chandam is the family name, Nicky the personal name, and Devi signifying that she is female. For the past thirty years, with the rise of 'nationalist' feelings, and the rise of many militant outfits, the trend of using two-worded names, with the first being the personal name and the second being the family name has come into vogue. So they have changed their names to Basanta Rajkumar, Nicky Chandam because even though 'Basanta', 'Nicky' and many Hindi (or for that matter Hindu/Christian/Muslim) names were acceptable as 'personal' names, Singh and Devi were seen to be remnants and constant reminders of forceful conversions. People who want to retain the three-word name format, replace Singh with Meitei/Meetei for males and Chanu for females. Not just names but there are other perceived similarities with the Korean culture. One of the armed group's ideologues explained to me how Manipur's Sanamahism or the pre-Hindu religion is a counterpart to Shamanism or the worship of spirits in Korea.

But what was visible was the Korean influence amongst the youth. In a few years the craze went on to impact the dress trends of young people in Manipur; a smattering of Korean words for 'hi' and 'thanks' became more hip. But in a family gathering during a ritual, the spiked-hair teenager easily transforms into a dhoti-clad boy and the girls play the demure role that is expected of them.

Manipur's appeal lies in this blend. In every facet of life here, there's a certain kind of fade-in and fade-out from deep-rooted tradition to strong outside influences, the blend between folk and classical and from the sublime to the grotesque.

Every now and then one can see that a group of women in faded pink traditional wear have taken position on the roadside or at a marketplace. The first time I saw them was at the Kwakeithel market. Placed in front of them were bell-metal water containers called ghot chaphu, similar to the kalash used for Hindu rites. It was filled with rice and a coconut placed on its mouth covered with bel leaves. It also had a bunch of bananas and the number of bananas must be an even number. This is an essential recipe for any puja amongst the Meiteis and it symbolizes the 'source of life.' It makes little sense to an outsider but one odd placard in English indicates that the group was protesting against some militant diktat. A few hundred yards away another group was mourning or protesting the death of a young person killed in an encounter with security persons.

Protests regularly adorn the cityscape. A fourth of Manipur is always on the streets protesting about something or the other. Eshei must have been much younger when I first saw those protests dotted across the dirt-laden city. Men, women, boys and girls were all taking turns to protect the territory of the state which the Indian government had obliquely promised to a dangerous group of armed Naga guerillas.

In 2001, these protests were so potent that the Indian government had to roll back their decision to extend the duration of ceasefire inside Manipur. This was seen as the first step in conceding the demand for integrating Naga-inhabited areas from Assam, Arunachal Pradesh and Manipur into a greater Nagaland. Manipur's integrity was protected by an unprecedented mass movement and the ceasefire inside Manipur was revoked though the Naga 'guerrillas'(which is a rather dignified title for groups of hardcore terrorists and organized dacoits) continue to push their cause and extort their own people, kill, abduct against ransom and when convenient, they claim their share of political power.

This history is very multi-layered and while it once caught the attention of conflict managers, it's no longer 'sexy' to report conflict in India's north-east. A constitutional monarchy, Manipur was brought into the Indian union by what is called an act of betrayal (disputed though) in 1949 and it was granted a Union Territory status in 1956. But Nagaland was given statehood in 1962-63 and it was only in 1972 that Manipur became a state. Insurgency was born in Manipur under these historical mistakes. The movement gained momentum and it was only in 1992 that the language of this ancient kingdom was included in the Eighth Schedule.

I've experienced a number of Manipurs. My first Manipur experience was driving through the valley in a faded white Ambassador car and seeing the place through the eyes of a poet who was on a self-imposed exile (and whose father owned the vehicle); a journalist who returned from the country's capital to start an English-language daily and a journalist-activist-mountaineer who had the air of a man who knew too much. He could predict what to expect at the next bend and often he was right. In one of our drives up a hill, he said we might meet some young 'revolutionaries.' We did meet a few of them and I am certain it was not an accidental encounter. I had no background of the place. Therefore, I was easily impressed.

I stayed with the poet and for the first few days, I hadn't even met the family I was staying with. Every morning the breakfast table would have a few casseroles and by the time my friend and I would come down to the dining hall, everyone would have left for work. The Chinese-made casseroles that were filled with food had initially taken me by surprise. They contained more rice than I could consume in three days. Fish, eggs and chicken, always accompanied with giant chillis. But that's a regular brunch for a Manipuri. In Manipur even social visits can be made early in the morning and 'work' includes a variety of social obligations. I am not sure why I was not given the usual tourist tour but I am so glad that I took the detour. It was more like a homecoming to a home that never was but one with whom I shared a strong, inexplicable bond – like a lot of images from one's childhood memories which are sometimes exaggerated or illusory. One of them was like the journey to a border town Moreh, a Manipuri Malgudi and then to Tamu, a small township inside Burma.

The journey to Moreh was memorable because of the terrain, the condition of roads and the adventure of being accompanied by a convoy of security escort vehicles. It was new to me but I didn't care, I quite enjoyed it. I cannot recall the details of that journey except for the fact that somebody's brother-in-law accompanied us and explained how to authenticate rubies. Burma meant rubies and precious gemstones for a lot of people. Even today, not much has changed on that route. We spent one night in Moreh, in an unpleasant hotel room with our windows open to let the putrid smell out. It was a terrible experience because hotels in this town were actually brothels in disguise and there were no other options. The linen was greasy and the pillow unusable. The night passed but the dawn came as a surprise. We woke up to devotional music from a gurdwara. It was Onam so the temples were busy as well. Moreh was India in a microcosm, but an India which India was unaware of.

In Tamu, I was shown Burmese rubies accompanied by a discourse on gemstones. I was a keen listener. Apart from rubies and other gems, bicycle parts were going to India. Going by the number of bicycle shops here, it would seem that this district exports one of the largest number of bicycles to India. The bicycle and rubies are all that I saw. But there was another precious commodity that was being smuggled into Moreh: a white granular substance called Number Four, the purest form of heroin, the deadly drug which would alter the course of Manipur's history forever.

The currency exchange rate was attractive. When I gave a thousand rupees to a bicycle repair shop, I got back three thousand kyats or 'K' and I felt rich. Beyond the borders of the town, we walked by a polluted river and stopped at shops to consume the contents of a green-coloured bottle before sipping and then gulping down some local brew. The liquid would help the alcohol find its way into the blood stream and was a preventive measure taken to combat hangovers.

Rows of houses built from teakwood bore no indication of a termite-eaten economy or polity. The elderly were seated on teak easychairs and the young were huddled near shops playing carrom. We walked up to the town square where curiosity at pro-democracy graphiti did not go down well with policemen in plainclothes. But I wondered why the posters were there at all; they could just rip them off. Twenty years later when the lady in those posters was released from years of house arrest, I recalled my first visit to the town square. I did not know of her then. Just a year before our trip, the pro-democracy movement had swept across Burma and the junta soldiers were making sure that their writ was imposed. Till recently, the country had defied all international pressure and indulged in gross human right violations. Women were raped. Her supporters were arrested as political prisoners. Monks were killed in one of the most oppressive regimes in modern history. But at the time, I was oblivious to it all.

The rubies didn't interest me, neither did the electronic goods. In the large market that Tamu is famous for, we bargained for a silk wrap-around, a set of chinaware and a large flask. I also picked up a carton of Marlboro cigarettes, a favourite item for Indians to take back home as gifts from overseas. It was 1989 and the guided tour by my Manipuri friends didn't include any of the political turmoil that Burma was going through.

A year before, on 8 August 1988, Burma witnessed the 8888 uprising, a national peaceful revolution demanding democracy. The uprising ended on 18 September 1988, after a bloody military coup by the State Law and Order Restoration Council. Thousands, mostly monks and civilians, who were primarily students, were killed by the Tatmadaw (Burmese armed forces). Hundreds of refugees spilled over and entered Manipur, where a generation of Burmese children are now growing up. During the crisis, the lady in the poster, Aung San Suu Kyi emerged as a national icon. When the military junta held an election in 1990, her party, the National League for Democracy, won. However, the military junta refused to recognize the results and placed Suu Kyi under house arrest. In 2010, she was released.

Almost two decades after my first trip to Moreh, its hotels and motels have flourished but the conditions have worsened. The window panes are gone. The beds need a desperate change but have been denied that little luxury for years. The mattresses are still soiled and greasy and nearly impossible to spend a night on.

Prostitution continues to be the most lucrative business, with a large number of girls coming from across the border, seeking employment. Each of these motels has an elaborate local meal arrangement which is their disguise during the day. Moreh is a very busy commercial hub so they never run short of customers of all kinds. Girls with sandalwood paste on their faces under a straw hat carry their kitchen garden produce and flowers to sell at the town market. They come from Burma. Burma became Myanmar and Rangoon became Yangon but Moreh hasn't changed a bit. The regime on this side of the border is equally corrupt and dictatorial but there is 'freedom.'

That visit occupied only a remote corner of my memory and subsequently, was used only as a conversation piece. When people would talk of exotic vacations I would draw attention by narrating my unusual Burmese excursion which included the gems and rubies, the market with chinaware, the sunrise to sunset visa we were granted and the one night in Moreh's seedy hotel.

I am not sure how Moreh came into being but one has heard of the great migration from Burma to India. The famous Bengali novelist Sarat Chandra Chatterjee, the author of *Devdas* and several other works walked that stretch. Amartya Sen spent his first few years in Burma. Amitav Ghosh too, has a strong Burmese connection. And the unforgettable Helen, Indian cinema's biggest draw during her time as the first 'item girl.' She was born to a Burmese mother and an Anglo-Indian father. When her father died in World War II, the family fled Burma and headed to Bombay; Helen had to leave school and start earning. At seventeen, with her first break 'Mera Naam Chin Chin Chu', Helen had already become a celebrity.

Marwari traders arrived from Rajasthan as army suppliers and they also set up the first petrol pumps in the region. They were then known as the Burma Oil Company. One of the first Marwaris to have arrived was Kishorchand Johorimal who came to Kangpokpi in 1926 to supply food grains. They came on bullock carts all the way from Rajasthan. Later they traded in clothes and plywood. They still live there in Thangal bazaar in Imphal. Even today, roads and alleys across the region are known as 'Burma road.' According to the 1931 census, more than a million Indians lived in Burma around that time. After the first Japanese air raids in 1941, the Indian population which pretty much made up the city of Rangoon started fleeing. Even zoo animals had to be killed since their keepers had left. Burma was pretty much in the Indian consciousness till both the countries swerved away from each other in a geopolitical tectonic movement. But the destinies of these two neighbours have been interlocked forever.

'History' is a very tricky and dangerous word and notion in the north-east. Scores of ideologues have given themselves the task of reinterpreting their histories written by British gazetteers, and inherited by what they call a 'colonial India' and its 'occupation forces.' Today there are many histories about these hills and valleys. Histories which reflect orally recounted facts and are often contested. In the process of witnessing the changing history of an erstwhile Asiatic sovereign, my 'motorcycle diaries' brought me to Paona Bazaar. Travels which began somewhere between Handsome House and Palace Compound. Handsome House was a tailoring shop in Paona Bazaar which later became a bookstore and a place where journalists, policemen and bureaucrats got together to share stories every evening. But that is history now.

The man who inherited Handsome House never had a spare moment and shared his optimism with cups of coffee from his Nescafe dispenser that worked only after he screamed at it in the vernacular. The arrival of the second cup meant that he wanted to engage you further in the history of his land, which is fascinating anyway. He would generously offer coffee in exchange for an attentive audience.

The person who occupied a small corner plot in the Palace Compound is the person who had chauffeured me around on my first visit and continues to work for a free-speech Manipur. When we first met in Imphal in 1989, he had set up a news agency from his home and he was sure of being in journalism for a long time. His focus was unwavering. From his agency he began publishing a newspaper, while I was scouting the front offices of newspapers in Delhi, requesting them to let me write a single piece.

The news agency became a signpost for any journalist visiting the state. He was literally bulldozed by government agencies but he took off for some time and then settled down to a dusty corner of the city near the palace, which had nothing regal about it. His columns never stopped informing a tiny readership of the goings-on of his beleaguered state. He was big and shy and almost always wore a jacket. He measured his words while speaking unlike when he wrote, and though he laughed and smiled very often, he maintained an orderly distance. A place is made up of people and not just the landscape and Manipur has a variety of them. There are actually so many of them that very often the beauty of the place is overlooked.

Handsome House is located at the corner of Imphal's most popular street, Paona Bazaar. Paona never occurred to me as a person's name and least of all as someone who determined the history of that state. The 'Handsome House guide to Manipur' too never felt it was important to inform me about the history of the street where I spent most of the free time I had there. So I did my own research into Mr Paona and it was not difficult to run into yet another informed Meitei who provided me with some historical background.

Paona's real name was Paonam Nawol Singh. He is better known as Paona Brajabashi (a colloquial form of Brijvaasi) as he lived in Vrindavan for some years. He is famous and an integral part of Manipur's history because of his role in the Anglo-Manipuri war of 1891, after which the British Crown took over the sovereignty of Manipur and ruled till India achieved independence in 1947. He was an expert in the traditional martial arts of Manipur and legend has it that there was no one who could match him in the martial arts, especially sword fighting. He is said to have gone to Punjab to learn a form of Gatka. Though Manipur had its own martial arts, it was prohibited at that time to learn or teach martial arts as it was believed that any person well-versed in these arts was a potential threat to the throne. Paona was a subedar in the Manipur army, but his incredible martial arts skills saw him being used by one of the princes to revolt against the king – he was caught and jailed. In fact, when the Anglo-Manipur war broke out in 1891, he was in prison.

Since the integrity of the nation (read Manipur) was at stake, and an 'outsider' was attacking and since there were not many able persons to defend the nation, the king himself approached Paona in his cell, made him a Major (some literature mentions him as major general, which is inaccurate) and sent him to the most difficult battle – Khongjom. Paona was perhaps around fifty or fifty-five years old at that time. As you might be aware, the British attacked from three sides: Kohima, Jiri and Moreh. The one from Moreh was the strongest and made the quickest advance. Paona, with a small retinue of armymen was dispatched; the Manipur army and the British met at the decisive battle of Khongjom, which is around thirty-five kilometres south of Imphal on the Moreh road towards Burma. Paona and his men stationed themselves on a small hillock called Khebaching whereas the British were already taking up positions at a higher range, barely 500-800 metres away. Heavily outnumbered and out-equipped, Paona and his men were routed, but every Manipuri valiantly fought to his death. It is said that Paona couldn't be killed even though he was heavily wounded as he was wearing a holy talisman which allowed him to choose the time of his death. The British were highly impressed and offered him a place in the new government they were setting up in the region; they attempted to win him over by saying that the Manipuris were no match for them and would be defeated anyway, why sacrifice his life for a losing cause, that they wouldn't like to kill such a brave soldier. They tried to convince him to surrender and serve Manipur, but Paona declined and was eventually killed. The British marched on and took over Kangla the following day but Paona went down in history a hero. Soon a bazaar was named after him. In fact the market complex – Khwairamband Bazaar, came about during the reign of Maharaj Khagemba in 1580. Later it was divided and named after the war heroes of 1891 – Thangal and Paona.

It is believed that a villager who witnessed the entire battle, narrated the story to the village and he did so by beating a dholak (not the pung-mridangam but the Pung Cholom) so as to attract a larger audience. He passed on the story by word of mouth to generations and even today we have the Khongjom Parba or the historical ballad of Khongjom, which is considered a form of folk art, performed by a male. It is also another dying art, with very few practitioners and with very little knowledge amongst the people, young and old alike.

But today Paona is like the Burmese market filled with Chinese-made goods that make their way through Moreh. Some shops make it a point to say that their products are from Thailand so that they can sell it for a few rupees more. For someone like me, every item was attractive: from an umbrella for ₹50 to a mosquito-repellent tennis racquet which came for ₹90. Fake Levi's canvas shoes, very close to the original design were less than ₹100. My collection of high-quality pirated Hollywood films and music videos were all acquired on this street. From Nat King Cole to Al Pacino, how can one not give in to the temptation for just ₹35! DVDs with nearly twenty movies! I was the Pirate of Paona Bazaar! A few shops had a variety of automatic toy guns and a collection of Rambo knives with a working compass attached to the handle. But the all-time favourite, best-selling items were colourful Chinese blankets available in attractive plastic bags. These blankets later started travelling to all the corners of the country so the flavour of Paona Bazaar has been compromised. But till the time Chinese-made goods hadn't flooded Indian markets, this was the only China-mall with an amazing variety of items.

The street would be teeming with families and guests of army officers stationed in Manipur. The state was never quite a tourist destination even though it has been on the tourist map. At Paona, apparel is also in high demand, especially jackets and cargoes. It is a really interesting walk and every item arouses curiosity – from punchbowls to cameras and generators to crockery. For insiders, the market was hugely popular for items such as the Moreh lace bras. Eshei, whose only fetish is lingerie, swears by Moreh bras. It's her Moreh secret! Also, 'bra' is a very important word amongst the Meiteis. Almost every question ends with a 'bra.' I was first exposed to 'Chak cha labra' which means have you had your meal? 'Paona bazaar chatnigbra? Chatsi Paona da' means do you want to go to Paona bazaar? Let's go to Paona!

But let me tell you about the Cuba I discovered in Paona. The one face peeping from belts, caps, T-shirts, trousers, objects displayed in every shop is the beret-sporting and stubbled Che Guevara. In red and in black. He is the most familiar face in a state twice removed from any revolution. Ironically the red armies of Manipur haven't quite adopted him, so thanks to a global fashion statement, he became young Manipur's icon years before his global demand. Chinese manufacturers have imprinted his face on virtually everything. I found a calendar with garam masala sachets hanging from the month of December in a rundown tea shop of a remote village which had a Che Guevara image. Badges with Che's face are available in the most unlikely places, such as an HIV drop-in centre.

Even Fat James' restaurant in Churachandpur has a Che face painted on the guitar standing in one corner for anyone to pick up and strum. Eshei picked it up casually and after fiddling around with the knobs, trying to tune the instrument, she plucked a few strings and then settled down to eat the Thai curry James had brought. James had renounced a lucrative career in big cities where he had launched expensive food joints, to return home. As the eldest son, he said that it was his duty to be home. I tried to understand his logic but couldn't quite follow the reasoning. Meanwhile, Che was sitting on that hollow wooden acoustic board. Revolution seemed inevitable! With his face pasted on camouflage caps, he is on every militant's head in the region.

A few years later, Eshei led us to a house in Imphal one evening. It was thundering and I remember recording lightning breaking the silence of a barricaded Imphal evening. It's rather tricky to shoot a sequence of lightning and thunder. The same place on the horizon doesn't light up in quick succession; the thunder follows the lightning.

Just as you mount the camera towards the east, the western sky lights up.

We entered a room cluttered with drum sets, guitars, sportswear and Rambo daggers. At the far end, a raunchy Christina Aguilera poster drew attention in the diffused light. But the candle light was reflecting off the eyes of the familiar stubble-faced man hanging on the wall. Hand painted by someone, this was not a Chinese import. The lead vocalist explained that Che symbolized revolution and their own music was an expression of their revolt against the system. This explanation was generated at that instant to impress us on camera. Or so it seemed. Che is definitely not a person or subject that is discussed or even paid attention to in Manipur. Even if one finds Che graphiti on walls across India in the Students' Federation of India logo, in Manipur the occasional graphiti still seen is of a certain Red army where Che doesn't quite figure. The drummer then explained that there is an abundance of unutilized energy in the youth and that is expressed through music. This sounded more convincing. Everyone wanted to revolt but something or someone was gagging them. So they either sang or squatted in roadside dharnas or practiced some sport or art or just went on with their lives. Che was a brand by default and the inspiration, if at all, was arrived at without any conscious effort.

When we left the house of the Che music band, three children were intently solving sums on a charpoy in candlelight. All Manipur evenings are like candlelight vigils in a state where there is no power, no running water but plenty of energy. There is no reason, however, for such a breakdown of basic facilities but people in Manipur have stopped thinking about it. It really doesn't matter as long as one is alive.

TWO

The Stick and the Pony

On a typical Imphal evening, I meet a reluctant nationalist. 'Typical' Imphal evenings are generally pleasant, dark and curfewed. Police commandos stealthily move in pairs on motorcycles through narrow alleys to kill people in fake encounters. Often, they make no pretence of an encounter. Sometimes they display stunts on the motorcycle, attempting to stand on the footrest with a gun pointed at people. Army convoys move through the main roads ready to shoot if challenged. They even display it in big bold letters on their vehicles: 'Do Not Come Close or You Will Be Shot.' The display is in English, Hindi and local languages.

On one such summer evening, we sat on my nationalist friend's guarded terrace where a young woman was serving us a cocktail of local herbs and fish. She was dressed in a tight pair of cargo pants and an off-white shirt. A camouflage cap concealed her face. In the scant light of the terrace, it was difficult to guess the gender but the person was conspicuous even in that half-light. Her movements were robotic. I was not introduced to her but I was told about her. My host claimed that she was a former explosive expert working with an armed outfit from which she had retired prematurely. This was her rehabilitation stint. She didn't speak. Her taut expression did all the talking.

Five years later, another girl, another explosive expert, was allegedly raped and killed by security forces in Imphal. She was dragged out of her bedroom and more than a dozen uniformed personnel raped her in her backyard and pumped several rounds of bullets into her. The story had many versions and was subject to additions and analyses; the effect was lethal. It triggered off months of civic unrest across the state and helped create another stereotype of naked protests which shocked the country: visuals of a dozen elderly women disrobing in front of an army post, carrying banners which screamed 'rape us.' The uniformed persons had no idea what they were getting into. The allegation of rape had become a natural extension of army occupation. It was also symbolic when the colonial Assam Rifles, a paramilitary agency which dominates Manipur, occupied the palace of the ancient kingdom of Kangla. But that was not the only issue that occupied the mind of the ordinary Manipuri. They had their lives to run and they knew it wouldn't be any easier even if the uniformed people left them alone.

Years ago it was on this terrace that I first tasted the purity of sekmai, the local brew. Tasting sekmai comes with a ritual. One has to dip one's finger in it and place the finger on a flame which will turn blue if the brew is pure – or so I was made to believe. It was my favourite anecdote for a long time.

Drinking any form of alcohol was banned by the outfits. Manipur and Nagaland are dry states. So our sekmai initiation was a covert operation. Dry states have a parallel economy of bootlegging liquor supplied by armed personnel which is similar to 'fauji tel', fuel illegally sold by the security forces. That is another story that connects these states with the 'fauj': bootlegging liquor, fuel and even ammunition.

Sekmai is actually the name of a village on the outskirts of Imphal. It's one of the Loi (Scheduled Caste) villages and one of the distinct occupations of Loi villages is the brewing of wine. Sekmai readily agreed to a Scheduled Caste status after the merger with India while others wanted general status. The popularity of the Sekmai wine goes beyond the state. It's a favourite home-brew even for people who have visited Manipur just once and they love going back to that taste.

But Eshei gave me a different story about sekmai. The sekmai brew Chamelei was made popular thanks to a hit Manipuri number by a singer named Naba Volcano. He was called Volcano because of his voice.What I also learnt is that Sekmai is a village which has produced several footballers playing in various clubs across India. Perhaps they produced just a few but the image has stuck. Each leikai or locality of the place has a character imposed on them. I have my own images and conveniently replace one with another. So while Sekmai is Manipur's vineyard, it is also the village of footballer Reneddy Singh.

Manipur is considered to be India's sports powerhouse and it is no surprise that polo was founded in obscurity here and a breed of ponies typical to Manipur were used for the game. The polo pony can still be seen in Imphal but polo is not the favourite sport amongst Manipuris any more. The first European polo club in India (and mostly referred to as 'outside' Manipur) was The Retreat in Silchar in 1859. The first competitive match as we know it today is also said to be held there in the same year. The club is no more, but a commemorative inscription of the first match still stands today behind the District Library in Silchar. The oldest club, still in existence, is the Calcutta Polo Club, which was established a few years later, in 1862. In 1864, the Silchar Polo Club raised a team called Band of Brothers and they played in Calcutta. The ponies were taken by country boat. In 2009, a turbaned, dhoti-clad team played an exhibition match in what is now Kolkata; this time the ponies were transported in army trucks.

For a number of people, polo was and still is the most common introduction to Manipur. 'Polo was founded there' is a sentence one may hear from those who pretend to know a thing or two about this place. But beyond that, most will have nothing to narrate. Even insiders know very little about it. Eshei had no connection with the game and therefore, had nothing to share. But the origins of polo may help historians trace the origins of the Meiteis. Polo became a casualty to Manipur falling prey to the World War II and Patel's annexation of Manipur to the Indian Union. It lost state patronage and died a slow death.

The game was not called polo in Manipur. It was known as Sagol Kangjei which was adapted and adopted as polo. Sagol means pony and Kangjei is a game of sticks. In Manipur it's played with seven players each who mount and ride ponies that are usually about four-five feet tall. Each player is fitted with a stick made of bamboo root. Extremely masculine and vigorous, the game is now played in two forms – the pana or original Manipur style and the international one. It is fascinating to see how elderly people also ride the ponies and play the game. The players are attired in regal and indigenous dress, turbaned and they wear a dhoti-like outfit. It's a white dhoti without borders, but it does not go below the knee. On his head the jockey wears a big white turban held by a khadangchet i.e. chin strap. He also wears a cotton jacket with short sleeves. The jacket and khadangchet bear team colours. Since no footwear is worn, the player covers his ankles with khunningkhang, a piece of leather or cloth held by straps. Above the khunningkhang, to protect the calves, he wears a padded shin guard called khongyam, also held by straps. It's a coincidence of sorts but most of this region is very egalitarian and the royalty is not separated from the common man. Polo is otherwise considered a royal sport, but in Manipur it has always been a common man's game.

A divine guardian who is known as Marjing watches over the sport. One of the rituals performed even today in the Umang Lai (sylvan deities representing ancestors) worship is a mime by the Maibi (priestess), holding a mallet in her hand, enacting a game of polo.

Mapal Kangjeibung or the polo ground of Imphal today is just another poorly managed stadium. But my interest lay outside the ground. Outside the stadium are rows of canteens serving the local cuisine. Polo may be a drawing-room introduction to Manipur but food is what takes you into the soul of a Meitei. In canteen number four, an ageing man in a spotless white dhoti with a noticeably thick roll of sacred thread on his bare body welcomes his customers with a smile. This unassuming gentleman was also associated with sports. He was the manufacturer of bows and arrows for players participating in the Indian archery section of international tournaments. His sons and daughters have been champions at international championships and now they coach youngsters after inheriting the makeshift factory in the backyard of their simple house. He could only utter 'namaskar' in Hindi but his generous smile welcomed guests with great warmth. Whenever I'm in Manipur, I make it a point never to miss his lunch thalis.

The story of sports and Manipur may have been stereotyped but unlike any other place, it is so common to come across a homemaker in Manipur who is a former champion at the Asian Games or a national champion in some sport.

Mrs Thokchom in her phanek, filling buckets from a tubewell in her garden looked nothing like a national archery champion. Meitei homes have a confusing front and back yard. They just have yards and very functional ones with a tubewell in the middle of a pretty flower garden. Mrs Thokchom's tubewell was right in the middle of two rows of chrysanthemums on one side and a large patch of yellow mustard on the other. Her husband was a hockey coach. Their children also played some sport. The drawing room was like a shop of medals and trophies from the entire family of champions. But they are so unassuming when you meet them in person. The lady did not hesitate to appear before us with a bucket of water used for the daily puja, which is compulsory in Meitei households. We waited as she completed the ritual and then began talking. There was nothing to even remotely hint at how she might have regretted giving up sports for marriage. Perhaps she had no regrets but I could not help but feel sad for her. The transition from being a national champion to a homemaker and with no fuss at all is what amazed me. She probably weaves her own phanek, cooks as well as her mother did and plays all the roles of a perfect Meitei woman. I won't be surprised if I see her in one of the protest marches someday.

When I first met him, Khundrakpam Pradeep Kumar was lifting weights at his friend's gym in a thatched house in an Imphal leikai. He was determined to defy the notion that people living with HIV couldn't compete in sporting activities. He trained himself to be a bodybuilder and in a few years, Pradeep was crowned Mr Manipur. Sports is so steeped in the Manipuri consciousness and comes so naturally that it was not unusual for even someone like Pradeep who took to doing drugs at the age of sixteen and like many of his friends was infected with HIV, to be active in sports. It is not as easy as writing this paragraph. He had to battle stigma and discrimination. Today, he is a subject for films and has a profile as a brand ambassador for the state-run AIDS control society.

Sport for the Manipuri is sacrosanct. Whether there is a curfew or a bandh or a riot in the town, sportspersons never fail to attend practice. The most ridiculous situation I witnessed was during a protest march near Kangla Fort when the police opened tear gas on protestors and I could see a couple of canoes in the canal that flows along Kangla. They had a competition coming up and in Manipur sportspersons are given all concessions.

Barring cricket, Manipur participates in almost every professional sport, from polo to baseball. I wonder how they missed out on cricket since a lot of cricket is played at the local level.

Recently I was exposed to a very unique indigenous sport – naked wrestling. It's part of the Kang Hi festival and meant to celebrate the heroism of the youth of Maram Khullen. The naked wrestling is a unique tradition of the people of Maram and I am not aware of such a sport in any other place or tribe in Manipur. Kang Hi is a post-harvest celebratory festival and the main attraction is the naked wrestling which is generally played out in the courtyard of the Maram Khullen queen. Although the sport has been in existence for many years, only recently has it become known to the outside world, because no outsider was ever allowed to watch it or film it. Maram is a small town in Senapati district, close to the Nagaland border. Khullen means village. 'Len' is suffixed to mean something which is newer and smaller. Now, when a village grows and expands into new areas, giving rise to a new village, instead of giving it a new name, locals usually retain the same name, but suffix 'len' to distinguish it. So Maram is the original village, whereas Maram Khullen is the adjoining smaller, slightly newer village. Sometimes, the original is suffixed 'Khunjao' (khun + jao = village + big), so Maram can also be addressed as Maram Khunjao.

Meiteis will surely disassociate themselves from this culture saying that it is a tribal sport. The lines dividing the valley and the hills, Meiteis and the tribes inhabiting the hills are sharp in some places but there are many points where they merge. For example, food!

Let's go back to canteen number four. Step in and take your seat in a classroom bench and table setting and a crew of young men with dhotis and a thick collection of sacred threads on their bodies like slings, are serving the thali. The ambience just doesn't matter.

The temperature of the chilli served with the food rises as you begin to relish the little bowls till you are driven to tears. They serve one of the world's hottest chillis, known as umorok. In Assam, they call it bhoot jolokia or the ghost chilli. This hottie has a huge following. A forest service officer living in north India makes sure his garden has a few pots of this colourful and lethal chilli. He also waters a garden of herbs he planted to curry his ethnic recipes. He has a story for every season and I knew he would have one on the chilli as well.

There is a wonderful story ... as you know most areas in Manipur are disturbed and many forms of security forces are deployed ... one new company of force landed in one of the hill districts; the personnel were out on patrol and came across a small vegetable market in the hills and one of the young jawans who was on his first trip, saw the bhoot jolokia and thought they were shimla mirch(capsicum). So he bought half a kilogram took it back to his barrack and prepared sabji of the bhoot jolokia. Imagine his plight when he had his first mouthful.

It's not just in India. The fan following of the chilli is led by Manipuris all over the world.

While visiting the forest officer's garden in Chandigarh, I met a friend of his from the army and there you go, he had a story as well: 'I have a similar story to share, it happened in Lebanon. During last few days before we were about to come to India, the Assam regiment came there to relieve us. My post comprised thirty troops. Thirty guys from the north-east came, mostly from Manipur. I got to spend ten wonderful days with them. And they brought dried pork, dried beef, dried soyabean, dried yongchaks and umorok fresh in bottles as well as dried ones. So, one day I was cooking pork and umorok metpa, which is a chutney of the hot chilli. My post-JCO, junior commissioned officer, a Garhwali, from Uttaranchal, came and looked at our umorock. We told him about its lethal power but he refused to believe us. So, he challenged that he could eat it, chew it, and he really demonstrated it too. For the next ten minutes, there was high drama to cool him down for he started dancing; his face turned red, sweating like a pig. He didn't know whether to cry, or to speak, tears in his eyes. We felt he was about to die. He kept on jumping for ten minutes. I didn't know what to do, I offered him sugar, ice-cream. That whole day, I didn't go for border patrol as well. I ensured that he was okay. Then, he realized the worth of this phallic vegetable. "Piglabasu champrane eikhoise," which means that even though we are physically small, we are capable of really hot stuff!'

People's Canteen, where I was introduced to Meitei cuisine, otherwise serves regular dhaba food. The traditional thali available during occasions or in the temples is rather elaborate. The thali itself is extra-large and the guest is seated on the floor. These thalis are probably hired for special occasions but otherwise a smaller meal is served on banana leaves. The bowls are also aesthetically designed from banana leaves. I can already imagine a few dozen Meitei 'Action Committees' formed to contradict this description and convince me how incorrect I am about banana leaves. In fact, there is a possibility that every detail in this account will be challenged. That is also quintessentially Meitei.

The list of Manipuri recipes can be long. They claim it is a south-east Asian and Indian culinary fusion with a Bengali accent. They have a lot of fresh vegetables with very little seasoning. Firewood cooking range is a must and has a perforated platform to smoke the ingredients. I love arrowhead fritters or koukha bora, wild sour apple sauce or heitup ambon, and gathered wild greens rice or ooti asangba (a gravy cooked either with green or white peas, lentils, vegetables and fried red chilli). Eshei has proudly claimed that she knows how to prepare all traditional dishes. She adds that her cooking is tasty and quick. Both men and women in Manipur are equally familiar with cooking. The discourse around shopping of local ingredients and the preparation of the food occupies one half of the Meitei lifestyle.

The collection of rice is exotic. You have the fragrant white rice baked in bamboo called utong-caak chahou ang'ngouba or the fragrant deep-purple rice baked in bamboo known as utong-chak poireiton chahou amuba. Even the names are as elaborate as the ritual of eating. They generate some sort of a Tibeto-Burman soundscape if you were to listen to them rattle out all these names in their inimical quick-syllabled tongue. There is also hui-kap which literally means dog's cry: apparently the rice tastes so bad that even dogs cry when this rice is fed to them. Then there is taothabi lake red rice or taothabi chak and fragrant sticky white rice or chahou angouba. What follows is even more mouth-watering, chilli mashed potatoes with fermented fish known as eromba and this is an essential accompaniment to every meal. It has a smell and taste which I had to acquire. Lilypod seeds with chilli fish called thangjing ametpa. Thangjing is basically spiny fruit of a water lily family plant called foxnut, it's called nikori in Assamese. Ametpa and eromba basically mean something like a chutney. Manipur is never complete without Tangkhul Naga chicken stew called haogi yen chamthong and river shrimp fritters with winged prickly leaf and coriander which is locally known as khajing mukthrubi bora. The troubled ethnic divisions are forgotten when it is time for food. I asked Eshei so often how they create the colour in their curries and she would have a wry smile as if to say that it is a royal Manipuri secret and 'outsiders' were not privy to it.

Meiteis are food fanatics and they would refute my knowledge with as much emotion as they would if I were to get my facts wrong about their culture. So the safest bet was to share my tiny repertoire with the aficionados and I was relieved to find that I was almost there. 'Basically, you got almost everything right,' the forest service officer wrote to me but he generously added a few footnotes which undoubtedly is a prologue to the original text on this recipe:

Eromba: It is a chutney with an overdose of chillies. May be made of different ingredients but the common ingredient is potato which is boiled and mashed. Fermented fish called ngari (these two are common in most Manipuri dishes) and the specific name comes from the main ingredient for example – with tree bean (Parkia roxburghii), locally called yongchak, it is called yongchak eromba – with bamboo shoots it is called shoibum eromba and with banana stem, it is called laphu eromba, etc.

Bora: It is basically a pakoda and can be made from many ingredients. With shrimps – khajing bora – with vegetables like cabbage, brinjal, banana inflorescence, potato, green chillies, arrowhead fritters etc. You have the name of the vegetable in Manipuri, suffixed with bora.

The canteen number four doesn't serve this range. Their menu begins with chak or white rice and then two bowls of dal, mustard chutney, some herbs which smell of the deadly chilli and a bowl of thickened gravy of fish preparation. The pieces of fish are much smaller than one finds anywhere else. The gravy has a yellowish tinge to it and again it's deceptive. It can be rather hot. But if you turn to your neighbour's dish one is misled into thinking you can polish it off. Manipuris eat more than a regular portion. On request eromba, vegetable pakoras, fried fish and a mixture of groundnuts and papadam is also served.

Food does not 'belong' to any one community. The Bengalis who share a great deal of history with the Meiteis also discuss fish with detailed characterization. Most of us have something to show off but it's unlikely to evoke mass hysteria. If the talk of fish was left to the fanatics, they would probably include it in their anthem. Bene, a foodie I met online, went to Delhi to study food but ended up working in a travel agency for a while and pursues photography with as much passion as she does food. Now she only shoots portraits to earn a living. Bene's page led me to this spiritual world of food and that is where we got talking. Food probably is the best way to lead into a conversation with a Meitei. I had just fished out a bowl of eromba exhibited on her online album. The bowl of that slurpy gravy had instant takers.

> *I want to be a superman and fly over Ema market, grab all the stuff and fly back to Delhi. Haha thanks ... I need some comforting food!*
> *I can hardly talk, the water in my mouth is flowing. Been years since I last ate eromba or even smelt it.*

Bene grew up on the other side of the divide but at a time when the divide was marked by several lines. The divide was between Nagaland and Manipur. Actually, it is not as much as Manipur and Nagaland as it is the Nagas of Manipur and Meiteis of Manipur. It takes much more than the eromba to explain the divide but the chilli is a favourite beyond borders and ethnicities.

It's not very often that my Meitei friends called me home. It was a feast for my eyes. Sitting on the floor cross-legged with trousers on and completing a regular Meitei meal is an ordeal. The elderly man of the house was supplying us with a running commentary on why this menu had been chosen for me. His wife's role was to make an obligatory appearance and ask us whether we were enjoying the food. The man with a certain amount of pride introduced his wife and said that she cooked really well. He did not forget to mention that it was he who had purchased the raw materials that morning and that he himself had crafted the banana dishes and bowls. I was invited to lunch by his son but the father in Meitei households obviously plays a more dominant role in guest relations. The daughter-in-law who is a software engineer was the one serving us and beyond a few smiles, she was almost invisible. Etiquette demands that one must not chat up guests, particularly with the in-laws around. Conservatism and chauvinism is visible even to the not-so-discerning visitor.

I had taken a picture back with me as reference and Eshei had to only look at the picture and spell out names I could not have recalled otherwise. According to her, I was served paneer/sangom sana, dal/hawai, boiled vegetables with fermented fish and hot pepper/eromba, salad, fish-rou/rou thongba curry, boiled vegetables/champhut, dried fish/ukabi, chives cooked with potatoes and fried peanuts/maroi thongba and besan bari. And I survived!

Manipur's loss of its kingdom was made up for by innovative attempts to hold on to everything that they loved. Like the dance Thabal Chongba, Manipuri food festivals in many Indian cities were becoming annual calendar events. But social networking and group mail gave birth to things like 'Virtual Hoten' (locals pronounce hotel as 'hoten') where members shared food, photographs and recipes. The Virtual Hoten functions as a group of young Manipuris across the world sharing a common space on the Internet. It all started after an alleged fake encounter killed two persons in Imphal in 2009. It became a regular online community forum. Soon the discussion on politics gave way to that of food. Someone back home sent pictures of boras and there were hectic consultations about the best bora. Nambol bora was the favourite of the first group but there were many other suggestions. All the discussions were documented with pictures as well.

Imphal's most popular snack which is also consumed with alcohol is kelichana. The pick of the season were the chana from Nagamapal, RIMS Road, Khyathong and BT Road. Kelichana is actually quite a simple recipe of boiled peas cooked in oil with onions and marois (garlic chives). But there is a story behind it. A lady by the name of Keli started selling this and the Virtual Hoten managed to acquire a really old photograph of Keli selling the chana. The popularity of this chana goes as far as canteens in universities in Delhi where Eshei picks up her stock though it was apparent she didn't savour it as much. But consuming it is like upholding tradition and therefore she would do it.

In the Hoten, serious documentation was taking place. Manipur's history was open to theorists because all manuscripts were destroyed by the Maharaj Garibniwaj who reigned from 1709-1748 and under whom the kingdom embraced Hinduism. The burning of the ancient texts is called 'puya mei thaba' or the burning of the puyas (manuscripts, the word is derived from the puranas) or royal books. Fortunately, one puya was apparently saved by one of his many queens and whatever history is now written, it is based on that salvaged volume. Bamons (Brahmins) who came from Bengal had written most of the texts which is used as the source material today. Any research of Manipur's story is primarily based on manuscripts collected by a few individuals and whatever the British political agents left as ethnographic monographs. The India Office records with the British Commission has important leads. TC Hodson, Alexander Mackenzie and Major William McCulloh are authors of books on Manipur. Ethel St Claire Grimwood's *My Three Years in Manipur: And Escape from the Recent Mutiny* is an account by the wife of the political agent, Frank St Claire Grimwood who was killed in 1891. The accounts are very intimate and personal and are probably the best available sources of information of Manipur after the British captured the kingdom. But the history of a people cannot continue to be written or told by others. Interestingly, today if a Meitei is looking for Manipur's history, the best bet is a 'mayang' or an outsider's pavement book store.

The Virtual Hoten has had virtual fights over the origin of Meiteis, one of Manipur's many contentious issues. The weekends are generally slow in the Hoten because the tea stall owner is busy 'weekending', claiming that he has run out of tea leaves and without tea and the local newspaper, how can Meiteis sit and chat? This tea-sipping adda, running out of tea leaves and suspension of the chat over the weekend are all imagined situations, based on collective memory. Eshei is a loyal member of this online community and this is as addictive to her as the other social media she engages with. They also started the leipung adda over the group email exchanges: leipung is a mound found on kaccha roads in localities over which young and the old sit and discuss matters of local, national and personal interest.

Similar to the Bengali 'rock adda.' One day, the militants sent an email note to the leipung following which there was a bitter exchange of abuses.

There is a saying in Manipuri: 'Chakcha yuthak phajaba.' It means that good drinking and fine eating is the reflection of a well-mannered, cultured person. This clearly shows that drinking has been a part of the culture. So the Hoten started serving virtual drinks as well, local brews from Androu, Sekmai and Phayeng.

Besides the sharing of food and drinks and the occasional spat, the most happening days are when someone virtually elopes. Nupi Chenba or eloping is a major source of entertainment. If news arrives of someone eloping then there are informers and peaceniks and lawyers and the entire sequence of post-elopement ritual is played out in the Internet community. With the real Manipuri taken hostage by conflict, young Manipuris give themselves the imaginative free will to draw humour from impossible situations. The hotel or 'hoten' therefore houses an online community holding discussions on various real issues and imagined situations, sometimes in a serious note but mostly in a light manner.

While Manipur is known for sports, little has been written about their local games. Eshei's childhood games were of course a mixture of American pop culture and Manipuri traditions. They played Superman/Superboy/ Supergirl. Cricket and basketball came much later. The traditional games they played were chagasi, chongbi, or even cheitek kotpi to improve memory, thinking and observation, which are part of the oral tradition of Manipur. These three activities are still considered to be necessary for the survival of a culture, of a history that is considered to be lost to mainstream Hindu culture.

Eshei's favourite games were bondi-paibi (a loose translation would be 'touching post'): 'We run from one post to an opposite one with the amangba (amangba – impure, profane. It could mean a lot of things, all negative, depending on the context) person standing in between. It's a game like tag. If he/she touches/tags you before you reach either post then you become the amangba. Our bondis (boundaries) were my Kaka's wall and a tree. We would shout and scream while running to either post and run together to confuse the amangba. The elders, especially granny would scold us and drive us outside to play.'

Dhampa-spite or hide and seek and 'Fire' was another favourite. 'There was swa too, where there are two teams – the guards and the seekers. The seekers have to touch the spot – usually a slipper – without letting the guards touch you, not even your hair. There would be a big square with three or four spots on two sides depending upon the number of members. When the seekers touched the spot they shouted "swa" and moved on to the next spot and then progressed to the other side.'

For Eshei, the best game was one that they used to play during the rains: 'It's called phi-lotpi. It's a little like hide and seek. We would all have shawls. There would be one amangba and while he/she is counting we will exchange shawls and hide under it, huddled in a group, in weird shapes together. The amangba kid has to identify the people under the shawl. And when he/she gets it right he/she can join the group and the identified becomes the amangba. These are silly games but I miss them. We had so much fun! I love playing marbles too … all kinds; I still have my marble collection. My sister and I had this standing agreement with mom … that she'll call us only when we are winning. My cousins wouldn't let us leave the game when one was winning, but when mom called, they couldn't stop us even if they wanted to.'

She chased clouds like other children, trying to run ahead of the dark cloud before a heavy downpour, playing 'auto-rickshaw' on windy days by tying mama's ina-phee (the dupatta kind of cloth that married Meitei women wear).

I had heard about the moonlit dance Thabal Chongba which is similar to the Garba. In a rather conservative society it is one occasion when boys and girls hold hands and flirt openly.

Eshei's family was not very keen to let the children participate in this ritual but they couldn't hold them back. She had an amusing incident to relate, where her brother styled her hair for Thabal Chongba: 'Of course mama sympathized with me as I looked ridiculous.' He cut a chunk of her hair in front, his version of a fringe cut and said it's Sadhana's style and that was Eshei's Thabal Chongba style that year.This festival was so popular that women would tailor blouses one saw in film magazines matched with saris that the girls could only dream of wearing someday. Till the eighties, women used to wear saris (they called it sari-full) but now more and more are wearing the phanek for obvious reasons.

Thabal Chongba also offered the first sense of enjoying a little harmless fun. Eshei was very fond of watching women dress up in sexy blouses and unattainable saris. She and her sisters would never get to wear them on that happening moonlit night, so those costumes would come of use the next morning. Eshei remembers padding up blouses with scarves and handkerchiefs and draping the saris in front of the mirror. Looking at her own reflection in mirror and looking like a grown-up woman was a real high. It was also the realization, at least a begining, of one's sexuality. Those blouses would never fit Eshei because she said her breasts had 'forgotten to grow.'

But slowly the Meira Paibi or 'women torch bearer' phenomenon hijacked the opportunity for young Manipuris to experience a tradition that celebrated youth. The Meira Paibi are the de facto moral police of Manipuri society. These are a group of women who take up almost any cause and transform it into an oblique mass movement. They carry a torch or a mashal which is called the meira and use tradition to launch their offensive. Some would call it a women's vigilante movement. Paiba means a male torch bearer. The 'a' and 'i' or 'ee' distinguishes the gender. Traditionally, women have a higher position and respect in Manipuri society, cutting across communities. Nupi Lal (women's war or uprising) in 1903 and 1939 are events often quoted when women's movements are discussed. And the general belief is that whenever some misfortune visits the society, it is the women who rise to the occasion and control the situation, and not the men. Eshei disagrees with these theories and prefers to stay miles away from these groups. Most of her friends would agree with her.

Even though some armed insurgents claimed to have formed much before the 1970s, it was only towards the end of 1979 and early 1980s that the real insurgency as we know now, came into being. Before that, Manipur was peaceful and the only problem existing was petty crimes and alcoholism. Alcoholism, at one point of time, had become such a nuisance and a root cause for domestic violence that the womenfolk had to come out to the streets to face this menace. This was in 1971, when a group of women formed what was called 'nisha bandh.' They used to gather at strategic areas of the leikai or locality and the streets at night to catch drunkards. With time, the torch or the meira became the brand and the icon with which these ladies are identified with. They have moved on from fighting against alcohol abuse to challenging excesses by security forces. Their agenda was also hijacked by the armed groups and it was believed that some of them acted as fronts of the resistance groups.

Meanwhile, young Manipur was migrating to Delhi and other cities and they took Thabal Chongba with them. Eshei moved to Delhi as well. A calendar event in Delhi universities, this dance may not be as popular as Garba, but it's great fun and full of energy. The dance is a jumpy one and while jumping, strangers hold hands and get introduced to each other. Many girls prefer watching the fun from the sidelines because boys take this opportunity to get introduced to girls they have been planning to woo for years. Often they carry love notes and while dancing, pass them on to the girls with messages like 'I will wait for you at the gate.'

It was one such night when Eshei met her first boyfriend who came and took her hand and she actually had her first Thabal Chongba dance. She recollects events of that evening: 'My friends and I were in a big group, we went in three or four bikes. It took us some forty minutes to reach there from campus, we were very excited. I was in transparent shirt with a tight top inside and a pair of jeans. I saw all the Meitei students there, my friends began dancing. We all held hands together. Then many Meitei guys tried to interrupt us and hold my hand from both sides. At least that's what I thought. People hardly speak to each other, they would just smile. Some guys tried to speak to me. I don't remember all the guys dancing with me that night. A few of them told me years later, that they tried to dance with me or that they danced with me. My boyfriend was trying to speak to me for the first time, he was nervous so he said since we had to wait for one whole year before we got another opportunity why not dance together? It's just once in a year. I didn't say anything and he didn't say anything after that and kept smiling. I just smiled. He proposed to me after that, he sent someone to propose on his behalf and said that he loves me. I said yes only when he proposed to me directly but I was really excited when I was dancing with him.'A few days later, he tried kissing her on a tour to Tughalaqbad Fort. She turned away. At home she was told by her mother, that when a girl is physically intimate with a boy, it's evident from her body language and she unconsciously carried this myth even as she grew into an adult. She could never quite enjoy the sensation. It tickled her.

Conservatism in Manipur plays itself out in a rather peculiar way. Holding hands in parks is a taboo (not that there are any parks), but Imphal has the most happening illicit sex scene in the high echelons of society. Narcotics, swapping of partners and gambling is a staple for high life in the dark, bloodied nights of Imphal. Conservatism is also a peculiar word. Getting cosy in a restaurant can cause outrage but maintaining a harem will not. Mind you, the social custom in Manipur is a little removed from say Arunachal Pradesh, where rich people practice bigamy or polygamy. It's a traditional practice. Manipuri custom probably allowed polygamy till a certain period but just when one thought that the practice was dead I was told that it's still very much around in its modern avatar. At first, Eshei refused to discuss her experience. She grew up with the knowledge that her father had two wives. She had the best childhood and education. She came from a privileged background and her mother was an educated lady so obviously accepting that her father maintained two homes did not come easily.

Eshei offered an unusual reason for her father's actions.

She once said, 'There are some factors, especially in a society where you find the guys joining insurgency, some go out of the place and get married to other women; some are unemployed. The options left to these women are simply to adjust with the well-settled men.' But she added that this did not justify her father's actions.

I thought that this modern-day version of polygamy was restricted to the community of people in power. But Eshei's father was not a powerful or rich person. It wasn't easy for her to speak. When I confronted her about this, her first reaction was 'I hate polygamy.' She was a child when she first came to know about her family and it made no sense to her. 'My brothers and sisters never wanted to talk about it. My sister still hates to talk about it, my mom doesn't talk about it at all, she suffered so much. I have good relations with them. Yes it was because of us, because of us ... my mother said she stayed on. She didn't want people to call us bastards.'

I thought Eshei wouldn't like to discuss this again. But she had to tell this to someone. Just talking would be a step towards closure. 'In school I used to be very shy when people asked me. My face would turn red. Now I see things differently, from all angles. My dad and I have a special relationship. When they had problems, he would call me and talk. My mom thinks I'm always on his side. I tried to convince everyone that we cannot let the past ruin our lives.'

Time changed everything and acceptance just wove itself in. Like everything else in this city. Militancy, poverty, filth and corruption. Dysfunction was stalking the valley.

Polygamy also brought unlikely lovers together. In faraway Pune, Nunglen had reluctantly agreed to stay on for his post-graduation. Nunglen lived for flashy parties. Meiteis can easily make friends but like most other communities they also enjoy the 'ghetto' feeling and so Nunglen ensured that other Meiteis also joined him in the party scene. And then, one fine day, he met her. The usual rites of courtship followed. Thariktha was beautiful and unconventional even by Meitei standards. She would appear a little Korean or even Japanese and had a yellow glow to her fair skin. She smoked and drank in public. It did not bother Nunglen; he believed in a hedonistic lifestyle.

Thariktha too, had a story like many others of her generation. A story of half-acceptance of the tradition of polygamy: 'I want you to understand that it hurt like hell during childhood. It was also very embarrassing and we totally denied their existence or the relationship. I found it hugely unfair for mom, I still do. We'll never accept "her" and it will always be the one fault that marred my father's personality. The kids are innocent. Only in my adult life, I understand and maybe forgive my dad. Love or lust or whatever is a human weakness and I guess my dad was just a human being. I think time and age brings an acceptance and understanding of all things. Personally, I still can't stand her! One thought always haunted me … what would I have done if it had been me in my mom's shoes? I never want to find out.'

'I don't think polygamy's rampant only in Meitei

society or that it's only for the rich or famous. I've come to the conclusion that men in general are not monogamous but some are only more committed than others. Our king also had many wives … and the society perhaps accepted this better during those days, as if they had any choice but not now. It's always an embarrassment and these ladies are not that respected or loved. Resentment? There was plenty as a kid. People always asked me about my step-sisters and as we never talked about their existence, I felt totally humiliated. I hated it that dad spent nights at their house leaving mom alone, that he didn't attend our school functions. I felt sad that dad always felt guilty and helpless, that our family could've been much closer and happier if it weren't for their selfishness … or weakness or whatever … but it all really doesn't matter now. Relationships are so fragile aren't they? There was no confrontation and nothing can be undone. We just learn to live with them.'

Even though marrying more than once is looked down upon, as long as it's performed with rituals it is socially accepted though not discussed. However, the same cannot be said for extra-marital relations. If men are found to have illicit sexual relations with a second woman, they are sometimes forced to marry and the woman's head is shaved off. This is of course, an MP (Meira Paibi or moral police) injunction in the new social code of conduct.

When I asked some of the young people I knew about their impression on polygamy, they were quite candid about its acceptance in society. Which was kind of strange to know because this is something that is neither discussed nor is the average outsider privy to this custom. While the women were in agreement that marrying more than one woman is quite common the men seemed to disagree. Nunglen was almost dismissive: 'As for polygamy, unless you have the statistics to prove your point, it may not be wise to generalize. I know of only one instance in my neighbourhood where two wives lived under the same roof, and the man is my father's contemporary. Of course men have affairs, keep mistresses. But it has become hazardous now with the moral stormtroopers keeping a strict vigil.'

Every second girl I asked had a polygamy story: 'Yeah it's common. My dad has a second wife and I don't know if I want to talk about it. I'm real close to my half-brother and sister and step-mom but I don't think I like it and neither do I support it. I am very clear on about my stand on this – NO. I have accepted my extended family and we grew up together. Two out of five families in our place practice polygamy.'

As time passed, the innocence of Manipuri life was almost lost forever. Eshei had an uncle who would play plaintive tunes on his flute and all the children in that leikai would fall asleep listening to that sound. He is no more. That simplicity and innocence also left the valley.

Eshei scribbled in her diary which she rarely used and even rarely shared:'Those were the days … and then all blank. "By the river of Babylon there we sat down ae wee way … wy nu remember zion" … and now we shall sing the lost song … That's how we used to sing that Boney M track with our limited English. There was no need to understand the lyrics, many songs whose meanings I cannot grasp clearly till now. The music of my childhood was blaring loud from the gramophone and the big disc was fascinating as I picked them one by one, looking from all sides to see where the songs were hidden. No luck. Boney M, The Carpenters, Abba – I think we were the only Meiteis listening to English songs and we tried our best to mimic the sounds we heard, still clueless but carried on singing "Brown girl in the ring, tra la la la …"'

'Evenings used to be film shows at home. This was before VCR or DVDs, we'd watch them thanks to dad's projector. Laurel and Hardy, Charlie Chaplin were the favourites. There was no need to understand the language and we would all be rolling on the floor, laughing. I don't think there was television yet in Manipur. Of course not. That was a different Manipur, a Manipur that many of the present younger generation will not be able to associate with. Films on big screen, the likes of 70mm were the main source of entertainment along with the Shumang Leelas. We used to go for evening shows and especially the last show after dad got back from work. My memory is mostly of getting into the theatres, enjoying some snacks, the film starting and I would wake up at home! I would sleep even at Shumang Leelas and I stopped going after mama told me I was too grown up to sleep at strange places. I gave up Shumang Leela and gradually lost interest.'

Shumang Leelas were big affairs, it happened only once in a while. The preparation would start from noon. Each leikai would have a different flavour. The Sinjamei leikai had housie draws or something prior to the performance. It was performed in the Bamon mandap or on a makeshift stage in front of the leikai club. Children generally miss out on the entire performance since it takes place through the night. The Leela had different themes and stories. It's traditional folk theatre. Shumang means courtyard and Leela means to play. So its literal meaning is a play conducted in a courtyard. Shumang Leela as we know them today came into being with the staging of the first play 'Harishchandra' in 1918. What is interesting is that Shumang Leela is performed entirely by males. Even the role of females is played by men, and some of the actors playing the role of females are known to be so beautiful that they were often mistaken for real ladies. However, during the last few years as Eshei proudly informs me that some women's groups have started an all-women Shumang Leela. When it started it was purely dialogue-based, spoken in the formal language and depended heavily on adlibbing. Proper scripts were introduced in 1950. Music was introduced around 1971 to accompany the flow of the 'leela' by a live orchestra, which in most cases are the actors themselves, who took turns singing/playing instruments, when not acting on the stage. This form of leela is called Eshei leela (Eshei means music or songs). Nowadays, almost all of the Shumang Leela performances are Eshei leelas. Perhaps her parents' love for these leelas gave Eshei her name.

THREE

Eshei

Her long hair fell over her face and at the most unexpected moment, a smile would emerge from near her eyes. If she cried, her eyes would puff up and almost disappear; but if she smiled, even a hint of that would not be visible. She was almost always dressed in a faded pair of jeans and a tight sweater or a T-shirt depending on the season; she made sure she was never conspicuous. The pair of jeans she liked to wear was ankle length and colourful socks were her fetish. She was not sure whether she used her serious demeanor as an extension of her personality or as a veil behind which she concealed her emotions. Extremely austere in food habits and dressing, she easily found acceptance but couldn't quite accept her own people. That hesitation was written all over her body. She walked without any swagger or tilt, her hips did not seek attention. But when she wanted, she easily gave the impression that she had curled her curves somewhere deep inside her body.

Her spine held her straighter than usual as if to divert the gaze from her shapely torso. With her unusual attitude, she naturally attracted more attention than she deserved, but rejected most of them because she just couldn't make up her mind.

Eshei had just started working when I first met her. She was rebellious but in her own shell. Reticent but opinionated. Honest but with contradictions. That was my first impression though not the last one. She lived in a leikai in Imphal with her mother and her siblings but she also had a father somewhere. Her mother was working and the family appeared solvent. Her younger brother was demanding a Philips sound system even though smuggled Sony and Panasonic systems were available at the local market, at a much cheaper price. Indian brands were valued above the ones that came from across the border, not very far away. 'Phoren' brands were too easily available and were used by everyone. So possessing an Indian brand amounted to showing off. Living in a large house with a courtyard and an outhouse, they were not very much part of the rooted society which Eshei wanted to belong to, yet she quietly rebelled against their norms. I am not sure she attended the family rituals with devotion or stepped aside to be 'different', a choice that often becomes a stereotype that one is trapped in. Did she believe herself when she said she doesn't fit into Manipuri society or did she slide back into that society at her own convenience? This ambiguity of her persona was almost symbolic of the place and the people she lived amongst.

She was an avid reader and cultivated a perspective that allowed her some objectivity that was otherwise missing in her peers. Sometimes the mere mention of a word, a name, a conversation, strikes you about the person and you are immediately drawn to them. Eshei's favourite painter was Frida Kahlo and I instantly knew that it was something I could relate to. Her favourite poet and singer was Leonard Cohen and I was deeply interested in knowing how she allowed Cohen and Kahlo to co-exist within her conflicted mind. Her strong sense of tradition and folklore, her understanding of the crises Manipur was confronting did not clash with her ability to embrace different cultures. She was at home in Punjab, in Delhi, in Ooty (the places where she studied and lived), and then in a narrow alley of a half-constructed city where police and army vehicle headlights serve for street lamps, where water is scarce, homes are candlelit when the generator fuel runs out and personal liberty is dictated by civil society or gangs of armed nationalists.

Eshei's life was not like her contemporaries. She played with them but remained aloof. She loved the sense of being fiercely independent but questioned the value of such independence. 'I have always had dreams, my dreams are many and endless. The experience of conflict also shaped my dreams. After the firing days I was busy with my life, falling in love, thinking about my future, celebrating and mourning life's ups and downs with my boyfriends. The eighties were wiped clear from my mind.'

'In the distant city din, with men and boys showering attention on me, I wasn't spared from getting in touch with the angst and hatred of some of "my people." I call them my people as I don't know of any better term to refer to them. They called me "sister" and told me the need for revolution. But I was too involved in my own emotional revolution.'

Long before Eshei confronted the contradictions of life and of her 'homeland', another man, like many others from that homeland, had attempted to escape. I met him over cups of tepid sugary tea served in tea stalls that also served rice. In many ways, Ravindra was Eshei's male counterpart. They dressed differently – Ravi never wore jeans, let alone shredded, faded jeans. Like most other things in Manipur, his wardrobe was contained in a synthetic zipped-up big bag from China. Everything in Manipur including the sunflower snack packets came from there. His Chinese wardrobe had Indian corduroy trousers. A couple of shirts which he washed with Chinese detergent – Oso – and neatly arranged socks, a sweater and a tweed jacket. He had a woollen cap and a checkered muffler which was kept aside in naphthalene balls for the winter. He carried a red woven bag with a tribal motif and a Chinese umbrella accompanied him wherever he went.

Ravi avoided looking at anyone on the road, although nothing missed his observation. While speaking, he preferred to look down. This body language is typical of people in Manipur. They take their time to complete a sentence and during that period it's not necessary to maintain eye contact. He smiled a few shades more than

Eshei but he stopped short of speaking at gatherings, allowing others to take over. He shared this characteristic with Eshei; it gave them immense power over others, commanding a kind of respect so when they spoke, everybody listened. They spoke in short sentences and often intelligently and since they hardly spoke, whatever they uttered was greatly appreciated.

So in one of those small gatherings over sekmai and a bowl of shrimp, Ravi explained how during the 1960s and 1970s, Meiteis followed every new release in Hindi film music. His mother was a Dev Anand fan and his father liked Biswajit. Every well-to-do household tried to acquire a gramophone to listen to Hindi songs. It's another matter that Hindi is now banned in Manipur and though they still listen to Hindi music, they do it at the risk of being shot. Their ringtones are Hindi songs and music in private vehicles is mostly Bollywood music. But the militant diktat against it is very much there. During those days when radical forces had not yet reared their heads, Imphal was a cleaner town and newspapers would be left at unmanned crossroads with a small money-collecting can. To Eshei and her friends, those days would sound like some fable which her grandmother filled their afternoons with.

But her childhood had been anything but idyllic. Eshei recalled some of her earliest memories of living in Imphal: 'My maternal uncle came to our house one night. He was very unwell, with blisters all over his body. I must have been around five or six and I was terrified. I thought they were heroes and I loved the line the People's Liberation Army

(PLA) used – "Heroes sacrifice and the revolution marches forward." The thought of sacrificing one's life for one's motherland appealed to me. I didn't know the difference between insurgents and revolutionaries. I remember once there was this combing operation and my brother was home for his holidays. He was at our neighbour's house playing with his friends. His sneakers were lying in his room. Some of the army men got hold of him, made him tell them his shoe size and all to ascertain that he was speaking the truth. It can be traumatic.'

'Operations were very frequent during the early 90's. My mom would pack all our valuables and money and put us to bed all clothed at night so that we could rush out if required. My dad wasn't around those days. Sometimes, we would all sleep together in the same bed. God! It was scary. The army and the police rushing in together. A member of the house had to stay with them during their searches. Usually, my kaka (dad's younger brother) did that. Once, he was not there so my mom had to be there to accompany them. I don't remember if there were any lady police … it was terrifying. And that was the time when there were lots of reports of women being raped by the army. Nothing untoward happened with us but the terror I felt that day has left an indelible mark.'

After several years of living and studying outside Manipur, Eshei returned home, but her Manipur had changed. Growing up playing with a Loi boy in his tree house was difficult to imagine because children now played war games. Loi means Scheduled Caste, but the

Loi community claim that they are the original vanguards of Meitei culture while the others are mere taxpayers to Shantidas Gosai. Gosai was a Hindu 'magician-missionary' from neighbouring Sylhet who made the King embrace the Bengali script and Vaishnavism. The King not only adopted the religion but also destroyed the traditional manuscripts and imposed the Bengali script instead. Armed revivalist groups have been trying to replace the Bengali script by burning precious manuscripts in the Manipur State Central Library in Imphal as an act of revenge against the King and Gosai. Internet hate mail against Shantidas Gosai continues even today.

But Eshei was determined to claim a slice of that life and stay on to witness the growing frustration. It was then that I met Eshei, while she was researching the transgender community in Manipur. I had formed my opinion by then: Manipur was slipping into a state of anarchy but Eshei defended it vehemently, in an attempt to believe that one's homeland cannot be lost forever. Her illusory Manipur was matched by the pragmatism or maybe the sheer resilience of my other friends. Ravi vowed never to return. The owner of Handsome House was brimming with new ideas because he was confident that anarchy made for good business. The journalist was still proving a point to himself by upholding some of the values of independent journalism. But each of them had to compromise at several levels.

Eshei recalled one incident vividly. It was in Delhi, 2004. She heard that a woman named Manorama was killed or had died in Manipur. This is the same girl who the government claimed was an explosive expert, who had surrendered. She was allegedly raped by uniformed security men who dragged her from her bedroom at night.'I read about it but there wasn't much in the newspaper that landed on my balcony every morning with a thud. The newspaper man with the bicycle was extraordinarily talented at aiming each balcony with precision. Often he would throw the rolled up newspaper without even slowing down and I marvelled at his skill. I was staying with my relatives then and people kept coming over. Women came, ate, talked and left for their destination: probably towards Jantar Mantar where everyone converged to protest. I also accompanied them a couple of times. I imagined that I was interested in helping the cause, so I distributed posters at Dilli Haat, or asked people to come for a rally march. I went for such rallies at least twice while I lived in Delhi.'

'The first one was in 2001 when the territorial integrity issue was being discussed. The Naga insurgents wanted the Indian government to chop parts of Manipur and other states for the creation of a "Greater Nagaland." The Meiteis were up in arms, refusing to part with even an inch. *Ceasefire!* The word dominated every drawing room discussion, while taking walks, in chat rooms, over dinner. "Ceasefire" was everywhere those days. I didn't even know how many districts there were in Manipur. The geography I studied taught me how many states there were in India, capital of those states, about rocks, atmosphere, but the physical structure or image of Manipur was hard to imagine. As a child, my sister used to tell me Manipur is easy to draw. It's like a left hand, I think.'

'So the idea of ceasefire and Greater Nagaland was inconceivable. Yet I went for rallies, shouted slogans and fought with the policeman who hit my friend with his baton. In the crowd, I too felt protective about Manipur. It all seemed so surreal. The next protest? No, I can't recall. But I took part sincerely as if the cause was the most important to me. But today I can't even remember what the cause was! I was sunburnt, my voice became hoarse, I developed body aches and I was dehydrated.'

Eshei had a long, steady relationship with someone from north India whose family had a large estate. His family found it bizarre that their high-caste son would marry a 'tribal' (even though he tried explaining that she was a high-caste Hindu). Like a good son, he conveyed to her that his father approved of them having 'fun' if they wanted, but he must marry within his caste and community. He wished to agree with his parents. Eshei's muted anger against this insult made her seek refuge in a female colleague. Even before she realized it, they were dating.

'Sometime towards the end of 2004, I was returning to my apartment with my then-girlfriend when we were at a traffic light near Jantar Mantar. The traffic slowed down because there were some protestors. Hassled pedestrians were irritated. My girlfriend said, "These people are like pests. Why can't they go back to their place and protest?" I am sure she never imagined that I would react or even notice her comment. That was the first time I was provoked and I called her "you people" and referred to the protestors as "my people." I don't know who "they" were. But the fact that "they" were harassed and were asking for peace and right to secure living made me bond with "them." Maybe they were Tibetans. I saw some monks too. My girlfriend could not understand my reaction. I deserted her and took the next bus home.'

Identity politics is the favourite theme in this part of the world. Layers of identities have an uneasy relationship with violence and power and for groups with extreme points of view, identity politics is often a means to an end for achieving political power.

The Nagas said they wanted sovereignty because they have a 'unique history.' In Manipur, the clamour for independence was because their annexation was seen as an act of betrayal and therefore illegal; they harked back to the history of their Asiatic sovereignty. Tripura, which was a princely state as well, had been fighting against the colonial forces for their Tripuri indigenous identity. The story gets longer and murkier as we enter Assam. The bottom line is that every tribe, sub-tribe, ethnic group, community or even separatist armed militias harp on 'identity.'

Till the 1980s, 'identity' was a word that meant nothing beyond an identification card. But by the time Eshei's generation graduated, identity as a Manipuri or Assamese or even narrowed down to Bodo, became a sensitive issue. While growing up in Manipur, Eshei wasn't even aware of 'my identity.' There was no need. But once Eshei got out of Manipur, there was the need to prove 'Indian-ness' or not be mistaken for a Nepali or Korean or even a Thai national. The taunts of 'chinky' were seen as discriminatory. But Eshei never took such remarks to heart. She remembered seeing boys back home teasing the non-local ice-cream seller, calling him 'mayang' and pushing their carts with sadistic delight. Mayang is a casual term used by the locals to describe an Indian who is from outside the state.

An Indian doctor in America who spent a part of his childhood in Imphal still recalls the word 'mayang' with bitterness:

> *Memories of my childhood and youth in Imphal is a 50:50 mix of nostalgia and revulsion. Nostalgia, because the happiest and most carefree part of my life was spent there. I had excellent friends – Bengalis and Manipuris and relatives who created an ambience of unlimited joy. Our childhood was a lot different as others of my age will testify because the pressure of studies and breakneck competition for admission into college was conspicuous by its absence.*
>
> *The only recollection of the daily life I have is the one of going to school, returning home and after a hearty meal, heading for the football field and then jumping in the pond to get rid of the dirt and sweat (alas, I did not have the luxury of the last as I could not swim and there was a stricture from my grandparents who warned me not to go near water). The Saraswati puja was a real special occasion for us because most of the cultural programs were staged then. Travel to and*

> *from the school was a real adventure because the anti-non-Manipuri sentiment was fomenting then and we, the Bengalis, were targetted by the locals. So on our way to and back from school, scuffles ensued. We were shoved and pushed and were greeted with the word 'mayang' which is synonymous with the word 'dkhar' in Meghalaya. To be honest, these scuffles did not bother me at all and sometimes, I looked forward to it. It is quite possible it infused a 'ghetto' mentality and helped me overcome my obstacles later in life. However, things are a lot different now and pushing and shoving are replaced by bullets from Kalashnikovs. For me this is the only revulsion, because of the extreme lawlessness and corruption and violence that prevails now.*

But identity was purely an instrument of self-assertion, with vested interests. Eshei had various grades of friends. Samom, a senior NGO worker once lectured her on what the army and Border Security Force did at Oinam, at Patsoi and so on and so forth. These stories would baffle her. But with time she developed an interest till she confronted the inherent contradiction and hypocrisy concealed in the word 'identity.' A very outspoken social activist who talked about Manipur's freedom and right to self-determination and the independent history of Manipur, once told Eshei, 'Ebema (a term of endearment used by elder people for younger women and uttered in a singsong way), if only we can get Aishwarya Rai from India, I would not shout so much against India.' Whatever he meant by that was not clear. Did he mean India would never hand over Aishwarya Rai to Manipur but expect protectors of 'identity' to give up their identity for their own interests?

By the time this passage was being written, at least fifteen armed militias who used to be defenders of 'identity', had given up arms and were happy to drive SUVs and throw cash to live extraordinarily extravagant lives. The magic word – identity – brought them near-celebrity status and soon they were framing policies as elected representatives of the people. Their great sacrifices, greater than the deaths of several thousand people, would be acknowledged by our democracy which promises justice, equality, fraternity and liberty. Liberty to kill and extort anyone. Justice only for the armed activists. Equality for anyone who is ready to join them. Fraternity for all who accept their writ and diktats.

Eshei was just getting over her second breakup. She had two gay relationships and had outgrown her lesbian feelings; she was now looking for a male partner. Girls, she said, were very possessive and therefore, scary. Her last girlfriend had become obsessive and wouldn't allow her to mingle with anyone. She even threatened to kill herself and it was at that time Eshei escaped from what was perhaps more of an experimental phase than anything else.

Homosexuality was never openly discussed in Manipur. Long ago, Eshei's friend's aunt had eloped with another woman. Elders laughed and said 'they are immature, separate them and they will be fine.' The same aunt was then married to a man and they have two children. Many years later, Eshei asked her mother about it. She realized that her mother still didn't believe that women could indulge in any sexual activity with other women. Women generally are far more comfortable with some amount of intimacy with other women. Eshei would imagine that most girls show off their breasts and bodies to their roommates or friends. Men she thought, are perhaps more private or are less comfortable with their sexuality. Girls also hug and sleep holding each other. That would be unheard of in a boys' hostel.

There appears to be some amount of cultural acceptance regarding homosexuality. Nupi Shabis or cross-dressers take part in Manipuri plays and most homosexuals have been make-up artists in this state even before they entered this trade elsewhere. Manipur has the tradition of Shumang Leela where all role-play, including the songs sung by female characters, are performed by men. High society Meitei men often patronized their favourite Nupi Shabi and they are sexually very active. In fact, many believe that the AIDS awareness drive in Manipur went wrong because initially drug users were considered the high-risk group but the gay population was not acknowledged. The incidence of HIV in Manipur is one of the highest in the country.

Eshei still maintained that she just enjoyed being touched and felt by a woman, but couldn't see herself as a lesbian. And yet after work every day, she would end up at her lover's house and stay over, sleeping together and making love. The last night she spent with her was torrid. Her girlfriend lived with her parents and sisters,

but nobody suspected anything beyond friendship. So they would wait till the lights were switched off in other rooms. Till then, they would hold each other playfully. In the dark they would strip and caress each other's breasts. Eshei would bare herself completely but her girlfriend would strip in parts. The first time Eshei held her breasts, she didn't know what to do next. Her most erotic moments were when she was caught unawares. She would have still enjoyed the intimacy but her lover's suicidal tendencies made her run away.

Being home was not helping Eshei at all. She had lost focus in her academic interests and she was messed up in her relationships. The little smile that sometimes peeped from the corner of her eyes was even rarer. As luck would have it, she came across an American student but suspected that he was gay or bisexual. She loved his hair but was not sure how clean he was. Nathan was attending a drama workshop and expressed a strong affection for Eshei, sometimes massaging her neck and caressing her elbow. Her own physical attraction for Nathan put to rest her doubts about her lesbian instincts. She had finally got over women and now Nathan's long hair was falling over her face as they made out one hot summer afternoon, in an elderly relative's house.

Eshei felt slightly better, lying beneath the weight of a man rather than a woman but recollected that the touch of a woman was warmer and more sensual. A woman probably knew another woman's needs better and had perfected the art of giving pleasure. She learnt that men were not so giving

men weren't very sensitive to their partner's needs in bed.

It was 26 January 2008. Eshei was writing from what she called a 'stubborn motherland' which is Indian in almost every way but refuses to believe it. Her ex-lover called up from Delhi – she was shopping and wanted to send Eshei something. What would she like? She did not want to receive this call, but it was good in a way – it convinced her that she never loved this woman. Over the conversation she only tried to imagine the malls from where the call was being made, but in Manipur it was difficult for her to even imagine malls.

'The malls in my memory all look the same. And suddenly I thought it is Republic Day, shops are closed. So how would she buy, but then I remembered that she is in Delhi. The place where R-Day is celebrated, not banned or mourned. In Manipur, we are forced to mourn on 26 January, 15 August and every time the prime minister or president or some high-profile political leader visits. Whether we like it or not, some groups feel the need to boycott and call a strike or bandh. We have no say in Manipur's democracy. Democracy is suppressed here, by threat and by muting people's opinion. They are waging war, the "war of independence and self-determination" from the "colonial" India. But what about us? Under "us" come the common people who want good roads, a salary without different percentage cuts, drinkable tap water, electricity, good schools, security. It includes people who want their children to get quality education without having to leave Manipur, as a rule and not exception. It

includes people who want to go out for movies, plays, classical concerts at night after a hard day's toil. It includes my mother who would love to sleep peacefully when my brother comes back late, it includes my neighbour who wants to rebuild his old house without getting a "letter" from some "patriot." It includes those who want to do business and develop economic ties with rest of the world. The "us" clearly outnumber them and yet we remain helpless. The time has come to look for the solution to this helplessness within ourselves, be introspective.'

Introspection had started somewhere. Eshei's contemporaries Romeo and Thaja had started questioning the events in their lives. Thaja was forever attempting to rebel against her mother's way of life but realized that she herself would become everything she hated in her mother. Romeo, who had once sent a love note to Eshei in a Thabal Chongba dance, forgot to grow out of his dancing shoes. Simple natured but born to an influential and rich father, Romeo loved carrying guns but only to show off his collection. He found an escape route from an otherwise claustrophobic political home. Thaja, who was almost forced to join a political party and had resisted, said that she felt a kind of hatred towards the party, even though, in a sense, it had sponsored her whole life. She said Manipur had slipped into anarchy under these people. There were no salaries for the employed, killings had increased and the party became a front of underground organizations. While Eshei believed in the same, she was more defensive than Thaja who was more rational and discussed her own family's unaccounted wealth as a symptom of social evil. Romeo was dismissive of politics altogether. He was pragmatic, but appeared more cynical. He did not believe in any political ideologies but had no way of separating his life from it.

'D-Day tomorrow. Will be glad when this whole farcical exercise of democracy is over. I think Manipur, especially our constituency, must be the most expensive to contest. First meet the voters, then have a "tea party" for hundreds of small groups (organizers earn a few thousands of course), then luncheons and dinners and public meetings, which all come to nought if every voter is not given cash (the rate is 500 bucks per head now). Well, that's free and fair elections for you! I think something's gone extremely wrong with our culture. And I feel sick sometimes because I'm also part of it. I don't think you can understand. Or maybe you can.'

To put it simply, this is an election in any part of the country. What Romeo forgot to mention were the threats from underground that dictated the terms and conditions of an ordinary Manipuri's daily life, during elections or outside of it. Romeo, Eshei and Thaja may have been questioning these practices aloud but were barely heard outside their space.

FOUR

Hard Rock and Roll

Martial arts didn't just happen to Manipur, it was passed down as deep-rooted tradition.

Apart from the few friends who I have already introduced here before, I think every Manipuri knows some form of martial art. Perhaps it is an exaggeration, because I am trying to do a quick count of the people I know well enough and none of them have ever displayed any martial talent. So maybe it is a little hyped. But it is certainly true several times over, compared to any other community. But this too requires some qualification. The Nagas would take offence if the Meitei dance is placed a notch above theirs, but honestly it's the Nagas who can deliver a dance performance almost anywhere, anytime with the right attire and adornments and audio effects. The reputation of their warrior race is defended with gusto.

However, the Meitei tradition has an aestheticism which I will deny the other tribal dance forms. This is closer to the classical form than the folk. For instance, the beautiful rhythmic movement of Dhol Dholak Cholom, a part of the 250-year-old Vaishnavaite classical dance form Pung Cholom, came from martial arts. A group of dancers somersaulting in the air, while playing the drums and in perfect sync. It is performed with grace and incredible skill.

Before the string of dancers swirled in the air, there was a prelude, a solo performance at the Bhagyachandra Open Air Theatre. It was at the beginning of 2007 and I was alone in the audience. I stood awestruck as the drummer hit the drums with his sticks and did multiple somersaults. He hit the drums in rhythm after turning three-hundred-and-sixty-degrees, continuously drumming. When he finally finished, his face did not bear the victorious smile of a performer who had nailed his every move. He looked bored. I looked stunned as the drummer picked up his instruments and excused himself. He was getting late for work. He worked at the post office and his shift would start soon.

What I find even more amazing are the scores of young men who apply sandalwood paste on their forehead and nasal ridge and wear dhotis to learn this art from various practicing gurus – they also slip into a pair of Levi's and sing Joe Cocker if you want. The other troupe of dance drummers who performed the acrobatics bowed before their guru, folded their headgear and dhoti neatly and rode off on motorbikes. Disciples start young and follow the guru-shishya tradition. The guru doesn't charge any fee and the troupes don't earn more than a thousand rupees each for a performance. Yet there is no dearth of students. This is significant in a state where drugs and militancy claim youth every single day. Tradition and modernity co-exist in Manipur with equal ease.

There are 400-500 Pung Cholom troupes in Manipur. During the King's reign, dancers were given land and clothes – today there is virtually no government patronage. Yet, the dancers haven't deserted the tradition. Tradition is regarded and defended strongly. Some may have been adopted from India, but once they have been embraced, Meiteis make it a point to preserve it and enhance it.

Eshei had as little idea of the dance form as I do, but she drove us to a village where some performers were waiting for us in the backyard of a house turned into a makeshift dance studio. Almost all houses have a courtyard with a large concrete worshipping ground baked with mud and a raised platform right at the centre, sacred space for a tulsi plant. A steel or bell-metal bucket filled with water and flowers floating on it rest on this ground. A large shed acts as a 'kirtanghar' or community room and generally has ancient wooden posts and even a little carving somewhere, as part of the home décor. This shed is a popular venue for household affairs and activities. Wedding feasts, funerals, death anniversaries, pujas of various gods and goddessess are all housed in these sheds called shangoi.

The day before we arrived at our shangoi, somebody had been shot dead behind the studio space. A large number of young and old people, men in dhotis and women in faded pink attire were visiting the house of the deceased. With a death in the neighbourhood, it was not appropriate to perform a dance recital. So the entire troupe packed themselves in the rickety van we were travelling in and with apparent comfort continued a conversation in the vernacular. Eshei speaks so little that her translations were mainly monosyllabic nothings. Eshei had decided that it is better to speak as little as possible in order to reduce the collective chatter around us. It bothered everyone else and that in turn bothered her. But she just couldn't form a second sentence in her mind after she delivered the first. Instead her mind formed images and went on a tour and she would very often miss events taking place right in front of her.

The next morning Eshei took me to meet a renowned musician. She had never heard of him but she was so removed from most things in life, her ignorance was not unusual.

A man was seated, wearing a Chinese-made Harley Davidson hat and a Che T-shirt, tuning an electric guitar in front of a lorry under repair in a garage. Cha would win rock championships across the country and is still considered the founder of the first hard rock group of the country. For years now, music has been a thread that connects the rest of India to these north-eastern states and made people like him unlikely ambassadors of this region. Cha told us that even today, rock is a vital outlet for the young in Manipur and the rest of the north-east.

Manipur has about fifty professional bands and the music of choice is usually hard rock and alternative rock, music that reflects the edgy nature of this troubled state. Cha may be a rockstar but in Manipur one wasn't surprised to know that he played Krishna in Manipur's famous Ras Leela celebrations. This versatility is natural and almost expected.

While we were sitting with him, his lead singer dropped by for a rehearsal. Dressed in a faded pair of jeans she had the warmest, most unassuming smile. Short cropped hair, a fading blue sweater with the sleeves rolled up, she came across as someone who was just a passerby. She had just returned from winning a national university's music championship and was preparing for her law examinations. She sang hard rock and performed a Melissa Ethridge number soulfully; sometimes I listen to it when I think of her.

Please baby can't you see
My mind's a burnin' hell
I got razors a rippin' and tearin' and strippin'
My heart apart as well.
Tonight you told me
That you ache for something new
And some other woman is lookin' like something
That might be good for you.

On stage, she's electric. When I saw her performing, she was wearing a miniskirt and ran across the stage several times, singing in a high pitch to a packed house. She spoke confidently in heavily accented English, telling us how she grew up singing devotional songs. But when she was six years old, she found herself deeply influenced by rock.

The reality of Manipur was never far from its music. Therefore, Cha was the natural choice even as a musical icon. Cha managed another band then, and he believed that rock in Manipur was the peoples' revolution, it expressed their anguish. It's not surprising that there are so many bands; rock here is as old as the insurgencies, so music expresses the frustration of several generations' feeling of entrapment.

I hadn't met Eshei for a long time after the Pung Cholom performance and rock and roll phase. Eshei was in a desperate mood to shrug off her past, as well as her failed relationships and her self-imposed love for Manipur. She had to break the jinx that saw her floundering between cities and careers and men.

Meanwhile, the journalist with the coffee vending machine started experimenting with enterprise, and set up a school at a time when others were winding up their business. He spent a great deal of time explaining the logistics and financial viability of a school with start-up investment from guardians who could send their students for quality education. He had studied outside like most of his generation and perhaps, he hoped that his children could at least study in Manipur. Soon, his school was up and running.

Eshei might have had the same dream but we never went beyond discussing what ailed Manipur. Her love for her people and the land was similar to the intensity she felt in her personal relationships. She just couldn't express her feelings. But expression can also be stereotyped and she was expected to perform in a manner that most people are used to. She couldn't and was acutely aware of it; therefore, her inability was accentuated with a kind of defiance.

Once, she shared a song with me called 'Nonglao Eshei.' Originally a Malaysian song, it is sung to welcome the monsoon. The singer is challenging the monsoon to come and revive the dry earth and plantations. The singer also warns the monsoon not to ruin the fields and and the crops by raining too hard. It invokes the rain to not submerge the langjing (hill) and wash away Patsoi Nurabi, the oldest village in Manipur. This song about the monsoon was her favourite, she said.

She loved it so much that she recorded this song for us, using a folk singer during the monsoon in a flooded paddy field. The phanek-clad singer was walking through the field, singing the number in a plaintive manner. Her long hair covered her bare back, wet in the rain. She appeared earthy and sensuous. Eshei's idea of monsoon was a synthesis of folk and physical beauty. The rain-soaked hills of her land excited her.

FIVE

Number Four

Shanta was looking out of the window and regretting her past and what may have been. A marriage that went wrong and then died. But nothing came between Shanta and her next fix. Not even if her children went hungry. She was doing drugs for a very long time, passing on syringes till she tested positive. That's when she wanted to kill herself. It was 1996.

By that time, a few thousand had tested positive for HIV. When we met her, we found that Shanta was not only HIV-positive, she had tested positive for Hepatitis C as well. A new health epidemic had been unleashed on this border state. Gender discrimination denied women and children from availing the state government care that came free of cost. It is never easy or convenient for a woman to walk up to a drop-in centre or receive treatment in government hospitals. The stigma was deep and not addressed adequately. Shanta said, 'I just remember praying to my god … "Make me live one more day" … that's my only prayer till today.'

At a drop-in centre in Chandel, I realized that Manipur's ailment was not collective. Conflict often creates opportunities to fuel addictions. Drop-in centres are uninviting crevices in alleys – drug addicts using syringes can drop their used needles and pick up new ones to avoid infection.

Luciene wore a wry smile as she climbed up a wooden staircase to the help centre. 'My name is Luciene, I'm from Chandel. I'm a widow and I am HIV-positive. On top of that, I have Hep C. My husband was an Injecting Drug User, he expired in 2004. Before he expired, I didn't know my status … I didn't think about it so much, life carried on. I have three children and my only daughter is also infected. Two-three years back I was tested and found that I am positive for Hep C. Due to my illness my family has not been supportive. I manage my own family.'

Luciene was working at the network of positive people in Chandel and earned ₹4,000 a month. She had three children then and her medical expenses ran to about ₹5,000 a month. Not surprisingly, she was always in debt. And she was not the only one. Others we met sounded just as desperate. But the contrast was Paonam who lived in the plains of Bishnupur.

Paonam's is a story of courage. Widowed ten years ago, she ran for the local body elections and lost it by just fourteen votes. But now Hep C came in her way. Paonam was running out of money. It would be the last day at school for her daughter Nungshi, if she failed to pay her fees. But Paonam had no money and no hope that she could manage some.

This is a difficult chapter of my life in the north-east. It involves several people who have been part of an intimate, personal conflict. I did not leave New Delhi for any great love for this region. I left to escape my daily demons, but they caught up with me. In the course of these two events, the region's complexities ran parallel to my own. For me, Paonam was an escape. To Paonam, I was a glimmer of hope. Shanta, Luciene and Paonam's hope against hope reflected the inner struggle of the people. In comparison, my struggle was an urban luxury.

Every place was the same. Each life resembled the other. And that realization perhaps helped a large number of Paonams to step out and confront the stigma and discrimination, and hope for a better life, perhaps even hope that their illness will soon find a cure. Manipur should have taught me the art of confronting harsh truths but my Bengali middle-class upbringing and confused racial stock disagreed. In contrast, Paonam's defiance and acceptance made one feel as if she had found the answer and she knew the truth.

A few years later, I met her again. She hadn't lost any of her spark; she was still smiling. She was accompanied by her daughter, all grown up and studying. With sandalwood paste on her face, a cheap bag, the magenta phanek and an off-white shawl, Paonam commanded far more respect than most of us because she refused to give up. That's the only mantra she lived by.

Tarun was never seen without a smile. He did heroin because all his friends were doing it. That was twenty years ago. They called it Number Four. 'It's a long story. As a child, I wanted to be the Taekwando champion of India. But then in the early eighties, in class nine, I was introduced to heroin. I thought I would be killed if anyone came to know. That was my fear. After a lot of hard work over the last ten years, I have learnt to live.'

As the virus swept across the valley, more and more people were finding themselves joining a fight; one that was never going to be easy. Every moment was a struggle – it was the choice to live with dignity. Stigma and discrimination were unrelenting, but so was the instinct to survive. In the tug-of-war between these two opposites, a community of people recognized that being on the edge meant a shot at a new beginning.

Ironically, HIV became a source of livelihood for several people in Manipur and the north-east. International funding was chanelled into the drug money nexus and a percentage of that went directly to militant outfits. The failure of the government at every level has allowed the militia to gain control. But if the government has failed to provide, the militants have hardly done any better. Their stringent tax collection bleeds every family, rich or poor. They demand royalties from each government fund and private enterprise. Each group demands a cut and there could be anywhere between ten-fifteen groups or even more. From Pradhan Mantri Gram Sadak Yojna to mid-day meals – every funding is taxed. The rate of taxation is generally five per cent on central schemes and three per cent on state government projects. Twenty per cent of international funding like HIV/AIDS went directly to groups like the UNLF whose annual budget is between thirty-forty crores, half of which is ploughed back into domestic and international investments.

The virus became a rallying point for lobbyists, non-government organizations (NGO), governments and activists. The 'positive people' soon realized that they had been identified as a commodity so they formed their own group. Layers of HIV politics plagued Manipur's black economy.

On the one hand, vigilante justice was being meted out to drug peddlers and addicts; on the other hand, the enforcers of justice demanded a share of that as well. The lethal cocktail of drugs, arms deals and a full-blown insurgency had paralysed normal life. The unusual became the usual.

Shanta, Luciene and Paonam's story travelled with me to strange places, where people knew them not by their names but by their predicament. Soon it would become my dilemma. Their stories were real and telling their stories did not necessarily ease their problems.

There were no sign of apparent decadence but things

were falling apart and piling up into a massive installation of waste.

A wedding procession steps aside as a convoy of army jeeps siren down the lane. Young men in spotless white dhotis, wrapped in shawls and women in woven traditional dresses or the phanek mapan naiba with gold ornaments bear such interruptions as a commonplace rite of passage.

A Manipuri wedding is a simple but tedious affair. Eshei was always drawn to the music band which sat in a mini truck and played wedding tunes. The 1st Manipur Rifles were known to be the best band in town.

Eshei recalls her memories of ceremonies attended or seen: 'The barat comes to the bride's place. The groom is then received by the pandits. The music hits a high note (it is similar to the tune of a brave soldier marching to the battlefield – I never understood why such a melody is played, though). But I've observed that they organize the background score for the entire event. They don't pick up any random track. It matches the live scene that is enacted in front of us. Marriage is such a dramatic enactment anyway.'

'The groom is escorted to the mandap by the bor senaba which literally means "one who escorts the groom." Then the Sankritan begins. Generally it is an all-women Sankritan group, with the only males being two mridangam players, the Pung Thingba, and Moibung Khongba, a conch player. The groom is seated in the middle of the mandap. He is not supposed to laugh or cry or talk. He is to sit still for more than two to three hours. I am not sure what happens if he doesn't obey these orders.'

'The bride is then brought to the mandap by the lead singer of the Sankritan – keina senabi or "one who escorts the bride." This is the moment when the music band blends with the Sankritan. From popular film tracks to Sankritan, it's a different kind of fusion, but so beautiful and seamless.'

'The traditional 'saat phere' also takes place in the Vaishnav society of Manipur. But there is no yagna; yagna is limited to the royal family. After every phera, the bride showers jasmine flowers on the groom's head. The wedding garland is also of jasmine which the bride weaves on the morning of her wedding. Young girls steal some of those flowers, because it is believed they will get married soon. I am sure the girls in my generation make sure they don't even look at those flowers lest they get married! But the striking element of our weddings is that with the exception of the bride's friends and young girls, everyone else is dressed in white. I am not sure whether the colour has always been white. And would you believe it, there are so many women in one place and yet no noise!'

'Anyway, back to the mandap. After the garlands are exchanged, the wedding is complete. Now the bride and groom seek blessings from the family and the moment of 'bidai' arrives. The background score now changes to a melancholic tune. I have often cried. It's embarrassing! It's live motion with full emotion!'

'Weddings also mean a mini car rally. Nowadays, fancy cars can be seen in the city. Till a few years ago, buying a new car ensured a militant threat but things are better now. The police band plays happy and romantic tunes, leading the car rally. Following their cue is the groom's car and then the bride. The bride and the groom don't travel back together, which I always thought was strange. The bride is generally seated in the middle with her friends beside her. The car is well-lit inside so that people can see them: it's a bit exhibitionist. The bidaai generally happens after dark. As a child, I remember rushing out with the sound of the band to catch the rally of vehicles and to get a glimpse of the bride and groom. Every child in Manipur must have done that.'

'In case the distance between the groom's and bride's place is short, the bidaai is on foot; while the groom walks, the bride is taken in an open palanquin. With the bride dressed in the traditional Potloi or wedding gown, it has to be an open palanquin.'

'When the couple arrives, the groom's mother and elders of the family welcome the bride. The band wraps up with a very sentimental tune and guests gorge on the food. The feast must continue, so after guests depart, the larger family and close friends feast at the groom's place and this is important since it is the first meal of the bride at her new home.'

There is always something sensuous about this place. The men look like a bunch of lonesome heroes and the women appear to be delicately sculpted. Their eyes possess an unvanquished power that has seen them withstand centuries of war and hardship. History has shaped Manipuri women into pillars of strength. However, today's Manipuri girls find this description ludicrous.

Six months after two dozen ageing women stripped publicly in protest against the Assam Rifles, a Meitei girl walked into a room to make love to a young army officer. There was nothing political about it. He came from thousands of kilometres away and had connected with someone. Sex had nothing to do with borders and roots. It was merely an impulse to feel alive and desired.

Even though the group of women protesters must have sat very close by, this girl lay on a bed, under the weight of a strange body. For him, it was like travelling in an unknown terrain. He was used to women with heavier hips; here he found sinewy bodies. Her breasts were very small but her nipples were taut. They appeared like eyes to him and he spent a long time under their spell. They were big and hard and dark and almost out of place in her slim body. Her legs clasped him in surprise. He was amazed by how she made love to him, with no fuss at all. They were two consenting bodies in sync. They made love several times that day. When she left the cantonment in an army vehicle, nothing had changed outside. When she reached home, all that lingered was a sense of great satisfaction. As she was changing, she heard that people were gathered in a house nearby – an amateur boxer had been picked up by masked commandos. She met him again and though they lay bare beside each other, that urge never re-awakened her body and she refused to make love.

Like in every other part of the world, people here were indulging their infidelities, they were having sex while gunfire raged outside. Normal human emotions were either suffering or maybe nothing mattered at all. No one really cared to examine sexual dysfunction of a conflict-ridden state. Lives snubbed out did not mean that other lives stopped living. They just worked their way around the fray.

SIX

Champions

Twelve years ago when I came here, a young girl took a pledge to sit on a fast against a controversial army Act, a dubious piece of legislation which has a pathetic record of human right violations. For the first few years, she lived in virtual obscurity of a jail ward of a hospital ironically named after India's first Prime Minister. Twelve years later she continues with her fast from the same hospital room, detained on charges of attempt to commit suicide, but is kept alive by the government; she is force-fed through a tube. Why hadn't I ever met her in so many years? I have no idea.

I never had the inclination to meet her personally. Maybe I did not have the courage to meet her because I was not sure of how a person can generate so much conviction. She has not suffered any personal loss but the loss of her people in conflict moved her to carry on the world's longest non-violent protest.

I finally met her the year she completed a decade of her fast. I assumed that her thoughts would be incoherent, but I was mistaken.

There are certain pictures of hers which are circulated regularly; the impression that one gathers from those is that her room is a small, cramped space with graffiti and posters and her scribbles on the walls. A tube attached to her nose, force-feeding her, makes one uncomfortable to continue a conversation. She is generally wrapped in a checkered blanket and a flask of hot water is placed on a hospital table next to her bed. She writes poems and also reads quite a lot; she gets a regular supply of books in Manipuri. How can anyone without taking a drop of water in a decade afford to think rationally? And even if she is thinking coherently, is the fight against the draconian act forcing her to continue her fast or is it that she has gone too far and therefore, can't give up her fight? Have her people for whom she has been fasting ever asked her to give up this struggle? Not supporting Sharmila would be tantamount to treason in Manipur, but the support is only a posture. Her struggle has been painfully lonely.

Sharmila looks back at the last ten years and asks, 'Why not? For me success is that very inspiration that I get from my surroundings.' She laughs: 'The positive inspiration for the upliftment of society.'

Sharmila's eyes and speech had no achievements to claim but she is aware of what has sustained her through an entire decade. 'My conscience, that's all.'

Getting access to Sharmila was not easy. She is detained

in a heavily guarded corner of Jawaharlal Nehru Hospital. To go through several layers of government and prison permissions took its own time. Honestly I hadn't even tried because I had never quite rehearsed this scene in my head. I had nothing to ask her.

I snuck in with two guests who had sought permission from the jail. The jailor was probably confused about my intentions and I took the opportunity to walk in along with them.

The hard-won hour-long interview was spent mostly in edgy silences. As if she was asking me … I am living the struggle … I am living my protest … what more can my words give you … that my life already doesn't? But all she said was, 'I want the Act repealed. That's all.'

Bound to her hospital room, Sharmila is freed once a year, a decade-long ritual in black humour. She is released for forty-eight hours on technical grounds and is re-arrested as soon as that time is up.

2 November 2000. Ten people waiting for a bus under a makeshift shed were shot dead by soldiers of the Assam Rifles. In the last thirteen years, the overarching theme in Manipur has been one woman's resolve to fight the Armed Forces Special Powers Act (AFSPA), which gives immunity to army excesses. Though the memorial of the massacre is covered with weeds and shrubs, Sharmila has become a symbol of resistance, unprecedented anywhere in the world.

Malom Village, on the outskirts of Imphal, is a nondescript cluster of houses like any other leikai in the state. It has been ten years since Ima Chandragini's two sons and their sister died in that brutal firing. Seventeen-year-old Sinam had received the National Bravery Award as a child. He was on his way to a private tuition class. His elder brother Robinson, a teacher, was accompanying their aunt someplace. All three died at the bus stop.

It was at Malom Bazaar that Sharmila began her protest. She had gone for a discussion on governance and when she got home, she was told about the incident. She took a bus to Malom and sat on an unoccupied verandah on the roadside. Malom was unhappy with her presence. They didn't want any retaliation by the army. They were numbed into silence. But she carried on. A day later, they say the police arrested her.

Eleven winters have gone by in Malom. During which one half-hearted inquiry has been conducted. All the Assam Rifles men who fired those bullets have got away without a trial.

Sharmila had an unusual childhood. As a child she would write poems on issues like social justice. In a non-vegetarian household, she would consume raw vegetables from her kitchen garden. As she grew up she started writing on gender issues while continuing to write her poems. Even today, in her jail ward at Jawaharlal Nehru Hospital, she maintains a diary. This is a poem she wrote in the beginning of 2010:

Who am I?
What am I doing?
Where am I located?

Who is making me sit here?
Until when?
What is it that they want me to do?
What is my vision?

Her mother Irom Sakhi Devi sits in the courtyard of their house with a stoic expression: 'I am a proud mother, but my daughter hasn't had a single drop of water in ten years so there is sorrow. Even if the Act can be repealed for five days, I think she can be saved. Just five days.'

Irom Sakhi Devi has not met her daughter since Sharmila sat on her fast unto death.

'I am a simple and weak-willed woman. If I meet Sharmila, that may weaken her. If she gives up her fast for my sake, that would break me. Every night I sit and cry. Every night. Just for five days, let the government repeal the Act so that I can see my daughter before I die.'

Sharmila may have been the defining image of Manipur for the past decade, but a lot of people out here feel that her determined protest may have been feeding the interests of other agencies, rather than pushing her cause.

In 2009, Meira Paibi, a women's rights organization, started a relay hunger strike close to Sharmila's hospital. There are a dozen others dedicated to her name. Sharmila continues to be the human rights poster girl for Manipur. When I asked Eshei and her friends about her, they vehemently stated that Manipur is with Sharmila. That was far from the truth.

Caught between human rights and inhuman wrongs over the last ten years, Sharmila has inspired a range of work; from films to theatre, she has had a number of organizations rallying around her. Therein lies the irony – what she set out to achieve is perhaps being overshadowed by the volume of work on her. Many tributes are prepared every year, most are weak and superficial. None carry the force to empower Sharmila's somewhat-diminishing cause. Candles are regularly lit at Delhi's Raj Ghat where Sharmila once escaped and sat on a fast. Men and women hold rallies, music fests, seminars in the capital wearing Save Sharmila T-shirts. Sharmila tells me, 'Let us realize why we are here in this world, how, when we will go away from here; this is our bounden duty to just self-realize.'

She reads the *Gita* every day and spends some time practicing yoga. As I walked into her room, she was lying down in solitary confinement, force-fed through a tube. Her satyagraha and search continues as she says with eyes closed, 'What is it that they want me to do? What is my vision?' But life around Sharmila's hospital ward goes on as usual.

Not very far from her jailhouse are women almost hanging from jeeps and rickshaws carrying their wares and produce, headed for the market. What drives these women to possess such a dogged sense of self-assertion is the stuff of legends. The ordinary woman on the road is as steely as any storybook character.

The Ema Market (Ema means mother), an all-women market in the heart of Imphal, can surprise you. From a seamstress to a potter, a vegetable vendor to a shoemaker, this huge township of a market has everything run by women.

Fish of all kinds meet here,
Half-smoked, half-dead, half-rotten.

I swear by Ema Leimaren, echa yokpa ngamdana mange,
I swear by my deity that if I am wrong I will not be able to look after my child.
They were just caught this morning from Loktak,
See the gills, smell it, smell it.

Plucked off breasts on lukmais,
Unsold like their cheap humour.
Dreams get drowned,
In the glasses of black tea.
Like slices of ginger and lemon,
Flies oozing their sperm swarming,
On kaboks, on honey, on the notes.

Women of all kinds join the noise,
Smoking half-smoked bidi,
Blowing smoke from the nose.

Smiling as fresh as fish out of water,
Wearing flowers in their ears,
With the scent of chinghi creating ripples of fragrance.
Poets say it is the scent of Mother Earth,

But they care not for the poets,
Nor for who sings 'Hallelujah'
All they care is about their guavas and papayas.

I swear by Ema Leimaren, echa yokpa ngamdana mange
They are not from Moreh.

They bring laughter from huts in torn thumoks,
They bring stories in red tomatoes from the hills,
They bring smiles in rotten potatoes and sour plums,
Tears leaking from torn thumoks.

In pineapple seasons,
Laughing at Bheigyachandra,
And their far-away husbands' testicles,
They sell pineapples,
In sarongs of all colors.

I swear by Ema Leimaren, echa yokpa ngamdana mange
They are as sweet as honey.

They call with their hands,
Rich gentlemen and say:
O Pamuba! I got lots of things to sell
Come, come buy from me!
This will be the first of the day
And you will be the luckiest in town.

Some whisper to others,

This man has got eyes like pineapples.
Others giggle and whisper,
But we got only two nipples, ha ha!

Hey bitch! Do ask your lady killer husband
To come here again (giggles)
Ho Ebema! Don't even think of him in your dream.
Do you see these Uhmorock? (they giggle again).

Altogether their laughter,
Their stories a noise,
To the ears of this city of villages,
But a single laugh is a cry.
That they can't save for the last meal,
A meal of few grains of superfine rice on aluminum plates.
The city dwellers take away their laughter in pockets,
The rag pickers dump their stories in their sacks,
While Bheigyachandra keeps looking,
Searching for the stars,
In broad daylight.

This is pretty much a travelogue of the market. Young Manipuris living outside have a strange emotional connection with elements such as a market. Ronid Chingangbam studied physics at university but believed more in his protest music. His impression of the market is one of the liveliest I have come across. For an outsider, it can take a long time to even identify the articles on display.

For example, the prickly vegetable that I picked up for its exotic quotient was disallowed by airport officials who saw it as a security threat. The vegetable is called thangjing. I don't think it is found elsewhere but more on that later.

Half a kilometre away is the bristling Nagamapal market which comes alive in the morning with a certain freshness which turns stale by afternoon, and by the evening, reeks of fear. There is a putrid whiff blowing in from the massive drains where mineral water bottles, carcass and rotten vegetables have intertwined on millions of pipes which never found their way to their destination. These pipes were meant to carry water.

Iram begins before daybreak, cleaning fish netted in the local river. She packs her trophies and catches a Tata Magic (the local name of the auto) to arrive in Imphal before Eshei's father chants his morning mantras. Eshei wakes up with the chant, but often that chant transforms itself into some fantasy, which she believes is a blessing from her goddess.

The same women who carry their produce from distant villages, often light their torch and reach the streets when people need to mobilize mass support. It's not so much of a feminist movement as much as being a conscience keeper to the society and a symbolic fortress of honour. The tradition has been hijacked by groups, outfits and other fronts and much of the valorous stories around the torch bearers today are misplaced.

The market was one place that made Eshei experience her alienation from the physical Manipur; at the same time, it was also one of the places that made her reconnect with her state. She sincerely disliked crowded places, and markets are always crowded.

After ten years of living in Delhi, the markets in Manipur were pushed back into some corner of her memory. 'I remembered going with my mom in our dad's office Ambassador car. I wouldn't get out of the car if we were at the fish market. I can't stand the smell and the sight of fish struggling in the tin containers that the women carried all the way from different villages in Manipur and parts of Imphal.'

'My mom is from a rich family. My late grandfather had fish farms and mom used to get regular supply of rare Pengba fish. It's rarer now. Another fish she loved was the Khabak. One look at the fish displayed, she would say, "I won't buy these Khabak. They are from Moreh!" She told me that Moreh fish are of a lower standard.'

'She was well-respected and the women at the market showed her their wares and tried to get her attention. I thought "Wow, mama's famous!" But all it takes was growing up. I realized then that my mama was a rich customer and that fetched her respect. Purely economic reasons!'

'Talking about fish, I was and still am very choosy about my fish. At home, I am very spoilt with my dad making sure that fish is cooked the way I like. Once, when I was much younger, my dad who felt that fish is health food, brought home some special fish. It was locally called 'porom.' Let alone eating it, I can't stand the sight of that fish. I was repelled at first sight. Dad insisted it will make me healthy. I was not convinced. Finally, mama cooked the fish but I refused to eat it. My dad had tears in his eyes. For them, fish is such a sacrosanct part of daily life that they cannot imagine their children not enjoying the taste. I was sad but I could not bring myself to eat that fish. I told him how the sight of that nasty fish scared me and I can't let that fish inside my tummy. Since then, he looks let down every time I refuse to eat fish and especially fish that is not fried. So you can see that I am not much of a fish person, which is uncharacteristic of a Meitei.'

'Going back to the Ema market, I don't have anything interesting to recall. The crowd and all the hurrying made me avoid market places. My mom's generation knew the women in the market and knew most of them personally. They talked about family, children, relatives etc. Earlier there used to be non-Manipuris in the Ema market. They were porters, most of them. But between 2006-2008, I saw these non-Manipuri porters being replaced by young Manipuri boys and girls. They were porters and used to sell tea, snacks and other odd stuffs. It was a planned change by one of the armed groups. There is not one aspect of our lives that is not dictated by these trigger-happy groups. I don't know if that replacement of non-Manipuris actually succeeded or not.'

'I love Manipuri food but the obsession with fish does not go down well with me. Actually, my earliest memory of food is of my grandparents. They were devout Vaishnavs. They ate only one meal a day, though my grandmom started snacking at night, but never a full meal. When Idhou (grandfather) was still around, both cooked for themselves after changing into their pure/silk clothes. No onion, no garlic in their food. No fish, no meat. We were not even allowed to make eggs inside the kitchen. Knowing that eggs had nutritional value that helped the grandchildren grow up healthy, my grandfather would ignore the fact that my mother was feeding us eggs. As a child, I was not fond of eggs either and fussed over food in general, so I often pretended to fall asleep while eating!'

'I love the food at home and during winter, I love it more. After a heavy meal, we would take a nap in the sun listening to some drama on All India Radio, every Sunday at noon. That used to be fun and whenever I got a chance, I would tune in, though napping is not really how I spend my lazy afternoons. Sunday meal would be ooti or chagempomba, kanghou and morok-metpa. There are different kinds of ooti and it's completely vegetarian. Chagempomba can be eaten either with or without fish. Its main ingredient is the fermented soyabeans which is locally called hawaizar. It stinks but is yummy. I have a friend who enjoys the smell of chagempomba on his fingers after a satisfying meal – much to the disapproval of his girlfriend! There's eromba and various kinds of kangsoi. Kanghou is a dry side dish. Morok metpa is quintessential in every meal. It is made from chilli and ngari (fermented fish). It is served in a small quantity, like achar, with Manipuri snacks, though there's nothing really that can be called Manipuri snacks. Some of my favourites are singju (various vegetables mixed with chilli paste and ngari with generous amounts of roasted besan and grounded and roasted sesame), spicy and super yum. There's bora too which is called pakoda in other languages. I loved going to a place called Nambol for the bora there. I would make guys who showed interest in me drive me there for sure. Those small open kitchens in the market where the people cooked are constantly busy. That's where the young ones sit for sometime and chitchat over a plate of bora and glasses (we say gilass) of red tea with a slice of lemon. Lecherous men loved sitting there, leering at every female. Plate after plate of bora fed their lechery and their non-stop chattering.'

'Food is very important in Manipuri culture. I realized this later. When we meet, our standard greeting is "Chak charabra?" meaning have you taken your meal? Of course, there's "Nungairibro?"that serves as a formal address. I used to find that really strange, thinking wasn't there anything better in our life than knowing whether my neighbour has eaten or not!'

Though Eshei generally kept to herself, on certain occasions even the most reluctant Meitei can go on without a pause. Particularly when it is about food.

'There is some eating etiquette. I don't know many but in my family we all eat together. Dad eats first, he starts and then we follow. It is quite stupid sometimes, but I love it. I wait for my turn but on days I want to rebel, I start eating first as a show of protest! I haven't done that in a long time.'

Eshei had been away from home for many years. But being Manipuri and living out of the state adds one more responsibility to the daily routine: to find out about folks back home. They are also conditioned to accept that news of death, abduction and any eventuality is almost foretold. So the Manipuri community even outside Manipur is close-knit and though divided into millions of opinionated camps, they share a common space because they all share the same anxiety and experience similar emotions of fear.

Eshei had called up home one day after she was told by her fiancé over chat that a bomb went off somewhere in her locality. Her brother went missing that day. Eshei froze as she confirmed the news. None of the rehearsals she did everyday over the years to prepare herself for such news came in handy. Eshei walked home, missing a few steps.

Her brother returned home later that night. He was taken by some 'revolutionaries' to ascertain his father's property in the village and was sent back with a finger on his lips and a gun to his head.

On another occasion, Eshei's sister disappeared. Her cellphone was switched off. It was evening and the family just kept waiting anxiously. The brother went searching at the police station and then canvassed hospitals. The family didn't want to tell friends or relatives yet, so the frustrating search went on all night. The following morning, an entire family arrived to apologize for the elopement. It didn't matter as long as she was alive. Eloping is not a strange custom here. A couple elopes and then the boy's family meets the girl's side, formally apologizes and starts the process of a formal courtship and marriage.

Eshei spent the night on a couch with white cotton

upholstery in a room which had no other furniture. There was no cellphone network available back home and the millions of thoughts that criss-cross an anxious mind were her companions every night. It was on this same couch that she had made love to him the first time. They dug into the couch just as the lights went off and left the couch as the candles were burning out.

A week later, Eshei was torn between a decision to return home or stay back when she discovered that her fiancé was cheating on her. It made her decision easier because although she was devastated by the incident, it came as a blessing because she didn't have to live through the dilemma any longer.

When she woke up, it was a Sunday, which meant staying at home. Her roommate in the working girls' hostel where she lived, was two-timing a French sculptor and a local poet. So Sunday was divided between eastern and western music, food and accent. Eshei neither displayed any affection or aversion for her housemate's preferences. She was too preoccupied with a cheating fiancé and a family facing threats from the underground groups. She could confront one while she had to silently accept the other. Confrontation did not necessarily undo the pain. Acceptance was far more peaceful. So, as the man she shared her bed with for nearly two years tried to explain his infidelity, it infuriated Eshei much more than a militant holding a gun to her brother's temple. She had chosen to spend a part of her life with this man and therefore the injury to her ego was significant. She had long prepared herself that he may move on someday on some pretext but to catch him with her friend was beyond her comprehension. The closest she shared him was with a stranger during a vacation. Though that was premeditated and both wanted to go through with it, it rattled her. She ran away from the situation every time that night visited her.

This time, she was almost on a verge of a breakdown when the news from home arrived. The boys with guns had occupied half of their country home which they said should be utilized for the sake of the 'revolution.'

Bad news can also come of use. Eshei's emotions were mixed when she landed in Imphal. What she left behind was a twenty-month life which was torrid and yet lonely. Now she had other things to take care of. Or at least she thought she had. She lapsed into a state of passivity and longed to return to Imphal.

Days would cross over into nights, Eshei would stay awake. Masturbation did not yield any pleasure. The more she tried to move away from the troubled ecstasy, the more the barbs of her love life returned to prick her. She was battling the existence of several identities within one identity. As a daughter, she wanted to return home. As a lover, she wanted to hold on to what was not there. As a Manipuri, her mangled roots were stretching back to people and places she assumed she belonged to. As a woman, she wanted to feel more complete. As a professional, she couldn't wait to look ahead.

SEVEN

The Red Hill

Just like Eshei's reality was juxtaposed with her longing of childhood and complexities of adult life, Manipur's past and present was a fade-in and fade-out with real people popping out from pages of history.

Gourmohan Singh was sunning himself in his courtyard verandah, on a synthetic mat which has replaced the earlier woven ones. Just like everything else, the mat must have come from China via Moreh at some ridiculously low price. A couple of other mats were rolled up in case visitors dropped by. His wrinkles were visible and his age apparent. At first glance, his face bore no stories, but Gourmohan could be a great storyteller.

The village is Maibam Lotpaching.

He couldn't remember the exact date but he recalled the time. It was a little past midnight. Hundreds of Japanese soldiers were arriving on foot. Gourmohan had gone into hiding when all the families were being evacuated and trenches were dug along his courtyard. The same courtyard where we were now sitting. The seventy-four-year-old Taoram Gourmohan Singh was a young boy, all of eleven, when the Japanese army fell upon the main Allied advance base in Imphal. That was April 1944. The war was right at his doorstep. On the Red Hill.

His memory was betraying him and his story was sketchy: 'I was twelve then when the war began … there were 300 Japanese soldiers on this hill … they reached at midnight on 20 May … they first fought in Moreh but couldn't come to Imphal … so they took this route.'

Suddenly Gourmohan rose from his mat and led us to a machang in the backyard of his house, or what was the original thatched home. He was suddenly energetic, pulling a bamboo ladder and climbed up to an attic. From a secret chamber which he had designed in his childhood, he pulled out a couple of ammunition boxes full of souvenirs which he tucked away so carefully for years. Rusted, but very close to his heart. 'I love these articles. Japan had come for India's independence, fighting against the British, so I keep them with me. I treasure them.'

He laid them out in the courtyard. Bullet shells, helmets and water flasks. The helmets had chinks on them and were probably the only remnants of the battle of the Red Hill: theatre of World War II where the British forces clashed with the advancing Japanese army. It's believed that Imphal was as bad for the Japanese as Flanders was for the Germans in WWI, for here on the bloody plain, 50,000 of the best of the Japanese army were killed. And it was from the Red Hill, its supply lines cut off by a heavy monsoon, the Indian National Army began its retreat just ten kilometres short of Imphal, whose capture could have altered the course of Indian history.

But the defeat of Red Hill didn't send back the Japanese. They came as close to the railhead in Assam when they took over Kohima. Without the bases in Assam they wouldn't have been able to access a northern Burma supply route. In the north they had already progressed, sweeping over Ukhrul but Sangshak was taken over by the 50th Indian Parachute Brigade and that delayed the Japanese advance.

Kuosa Kere could speak a smattering of Japanese. It was at Kigwema village where General Saito, the famed Japanese commander had stationed himself during the decisive siege of Kohima in World War II. From here, the Japanese 31st Division opened attack and timed the assault at exactly four pm on '4.04.44.' It lasted for two months. 'It was a long war, we were warned by the Brits and were very apprehensive about the Japanese, but they were friendly. They lived with the families, paid for everything and unlike the British, they had no relationships with local women. They never misbehaved. General Saito was a very nice man. For us teenagers, the war was an adventure.'

It was in June when the dangerous Japanese advance into the plains of India was finally halted by the British and Indian forces. Sixty-four years after the famous Kohima seige of World War II, I stumbled upon some rare photographs and calligraphic notes documenting the most decisive war against Japan. What I found in those huge album notebooks were daily accounts maintained by the British 2nd Division.

There were several photographs but the ones in my acquisition were aerial views of the supply points in Kohima, Japanese posts, Kohima a day after the Japanese retreated, and British artillery positions. These pictures gave me an assumed status of a collector and I prided myself immensely on possessing war memorabilia, even if it was only three photographs.

During the war, China, Burma and India were considered an insignificant theatre but the stakes were enormous. Had the Japanese managed to break through the Indian defence lines they would have been able to link up with allies Germany and Italy to control the all-important oil fields in the Middle East.

In a telegram to Franklin Roosevelt, Winston Churchill wrote, 'The stakes are pretty high in this battle, and victory would have far reaching consequences [as would defeat].'

It was 22 June 1944, when the Japanese forces finally withdrew. But what went down in history as one of the fiercest battles of World War II was fought on a tennis court adjoining the Deputy Commissioner's bungalow in Kohima.

Kohima's new landmark, The Dream Café overlooks the 'tennis court.' This café is actually a time-zone as far as Nagaland's contemporary history goes. It was the first shop in Kohima to stay open till eight in the evening. Theja's Dream Café is a busy coffee house in the middle of the city, a place which symbolizes the new Nagaland – moving away from the stereotype of a Naga tribal dancer that graces the covers of travel books. Dream Café is the other young haunt marking a changed attitude for a beleaguered state fighting one of the world's oldest insurgencies.

Across the Dream Café is the Kohima War Cemetery, where 1200 Indian and British soldiers who died fighting the Japanese have been laid to rest. This is where the tennis court battle was fought and where the famous line is found engraved: When you go home tell them of us and say, "For your tomorrow, we gave our today." The tennis court battle was also called the 'Battle under the Cherry Tree.' The cherry tree was a Japanese sniper post. The tree is no more but a branch of the famed tree has taken its place outdoors, next to the tennis court, which can still be seen. Young Nagaland finds refuge in this tennis court now. It's a romantic getaway right in the middle of the town.

A British war veteran whose name I cannot recall stood in the middle of the cemetery and reminisced: 'After several months, it was virtually over. We were repatriated home; we were on our way to Bombay when the atom bomb was dropped. It was all over. We don't want it but we do need it sometimes ... hmmm look at this. It's the sad part, but anyway we came out victorious.' Tears rolled down his wrinkled cheeks.

But sitting at a tombstone, Lily broke down: 'Sixty years ago, I was a nurse at the army-combined hospitals. So many young people had died, too many lives wasted, they died in my arms. And we still have wars.'

Chuba lives on the highway from Imphal to Kohima and helped the Japanese; he also fought with the first Naga underground army. He now makes wooden army boots and eats with chopsticks, something he picked up when he stayed in the camps with the Japanese. Chuba is almost senile and sometimes seems to believe that the Japanese are still around.

Eshei is not exactly a World War enthusiast, but wanted to add Nagaland to her travels, so she undertook this journey. She meticulously noted down her observations from Imphal to Kohima and further down to the plains of Assam, where she spent a night in a circuit house with a musician she had met along the journey. This is one encounter she had nothing to note down about. She lay on her bed with a headache from hell and her bare body stayed untouched by a man who stood there, watching her.

The theatre of war had another location and Eshei would travel there as well. Eshei's travels and her notes had nothing to do with her work. She ran a bookshop in Delhi with a partner but spent a lot of time on her own. She was no longer under any illusion of 'discovering herself' any more than she had already done.

Regular vehicles wouldn't have been able to make it through that stretch. Eshei had to arrange for a four-wheel drive, a Maruti Gypsy from the nearby police station. To arrange that she had to call up her politician-uncle for help and even then the policemen had been reluctant to spare their only vehicle. It was a green battle-scarred Gypsy which had borne witness to an unknown number of encounters with armed groups.

The road was apparently safe, but was heavy with an air of uneasiness. 'Safe' has various connotations in these parts. For example, in Manipur, if you are not shot dead or abducted, then you are considered safe. In Nagaland too, it's more or less the same. In Arunachal Pradesh, you are safe as long as you haven't lost your way or got caught in some landslide or stranded in some town till the weather clears up and the outside world evacuates the place. This was a road leading from Assam to Arunachal Pradesh and into Myanmar. Comparatively safe, but this historical road is fraught with a danger that's quite palpable. There are at least thirteen army, police and paramilitary barricades where personal identity cards have to be displayed. However, militants always stick to the jungle path. It's easier. Security persons very rarely venture there because of a mutually agreed treaty. Abductions of travellers like Eshei are uncommon in these areas. Or even being ambushed by dacoits. But something is not quite right on these roads. Things can go awry.

The map Eshei spreads out on the bumpy ride marks the Indo-Myanmar border in Arunachal Pradesh, a stretch that runs more than 1600 kilometres and passes of 9000 feet in the Patkai range. It's through these high passes that tribes such as the Singhpos crossed over from China to India in the thirteenth century. The Singhpos gave tea to the world; incidentally Eshei's ancestry is also from China.

Prince Sukapha from Thailand is believed to have

galloped down this route and set up the Ahom dynasty which reigned over Assam and Nagaland for 600 years, even longer than the Mughal dynasty.

Eshei stood on the road which was once the lifeline for the Allied Forces during World War II. Most of this area along the border is virtually pathless. Malarial mosquitoes thrive and the climate is hellishly humid. Incessant rains drench the highlands of Arunachal Pradesh, with Myanmar and Bhutan's rainforests lying to the east and west, the frigid Tibetan plateau to the north and the Brahmaputra's sweltering lowlands in the south.

Parts of a World War II jeep and a gas pipeline, laid when the road was built, are visible but only if the foliage is removed. But rainforests are dangerous to explore. The trees are so tall that they actually reach the sky. They have wide trunks that look like a woman dressed in a wraparound on a windy day. The leaves are large and the branches are unreachable. The forest has a mysterious, unattainable kind of beauty and nature is so indifferent to what she inspires. Eshei studied the rainforest trees but it's not fun to be surrounded by leeches that leap on you from those trees. There is always moisture in the air. The worst stretch was from Nampong to the Pangsau Pass, under a thick canopy of rainforest which has denied the earth beneath any sunlight for years.

Logistics is the biggest bottleneck for border villages. Ironically though, this road was one of the most astonishing engineering feats of WWII. It's the Stilwell road where the Allied Forces endured disease, monsoons and Japanese air raids to build the legendary 1800 kilometres supply line that still winds through three nations – India, Myanmar and China.

It's only twelve kilometres from the village Thirmkam in Nampong to the Myanmar border at Pangsau, but it seemed like Eshei would never make it to the Pangsau Pass through which Stilwell road runs.

It took her more than an hour's drive across the border into Myanmar to Pangsau village. A row of five shops sell Rambo daggers with a compass fitted on the handle, along with locally woven hats. Armed with a dagger to counter the leeches, Eshei was forced to return by the Myanmarese border police. In the distance was 'The Lake of No Return.' It is a very intriguing name and comes with an equally interesting story. It's not a stunning sight and it is not tempting enough to trek that far either. But the story of the lake remains fascinating.

There are several versions of the lore. When pilots flew across the hump (in war chronicles the 'hump' is rather infamous) they crashed into this lake. There was an airstrip next to the Lake and often tired pilots would mistake the shining surface of the lake for the airstrip and crash into the waters.

Locals claim that militants had hit on a goldmine of a pile of explosives under the lake. So according to this theory, half the explosions in the last three decades can be attributed to the WWII ammunition dump!

If malaria doesn't kill you here, then chances are that you may die of a bullet – caught in the crossfire between the Indian security forces and scores of armed Indian militant groups, who use this war path to cross over and enter India from Myanmar. For decades, insurgents were trained by the Kachin rebels and these outfits housed themselves in Myanmar. Even today, groups like the National Socialist Council of Nagaland-Isak Muivah (NSCN-IM), the National Socialist Council of Nagaland-Khaplang (NSCN-K) and the United Liberation Front of Assam (ULFA) roam around freely, carrying out extortions, cultivating poppy illegally and of course, harassing the inhabitants of these parts. These are liberated zones and the diktat of drug lords are writ on every turn of this ancient pass.

Khumlan Mossang was probably one of the few village heads in the two Arunachal districts of Tirap and Changlang, who hadn't signed the unofficial referendum note by the NSCN-IM; it asked people to join Greater Nagaland, composed of Naga-dominated areas across four States of the north-east. That's out of the ordinary but Khumlan was never nominated for any government award.

This Stilwell road got its name from the maverick Lieutenant General Joseph Stilwell and old China hand also known as 'Vinegar Joe,' who had set himself a target of constructing a kilometre of road every day. It is also called the 'man a mile road'. It starts in the Assamese town of Ledo and that section of the road is called Pick's Pike after its engineer General Lewis Pick. Today the same area virtually has no roads. Average distance between the villages takes fifteen-twenty hours on foot. There are places along the border where people walk for twenty-five days. Other villages like Bijoynagar don't even have a jungle track. Arunachal Pradesh is simply not negotiable. An acute feeling of alienation defines those who live along this border.

From the primeval forest with the monsoon pouring relentlessly, leeches leapfrogging in the tropical rainforests of Arunachal Pradesh and Myanmar, where south-east Asia meets south Asia – Eshei's walk through the rainforest forced her take a step into her own mind.

Eshei's consciousness was a riot. Nothing was working. Least of all, a grimy trek and police-jeep drive through a WWII jungle path. She had lived away from home for too long, and had naively imagined that home was missing her. No one misses anyone for too long. She herself had ceased missing her lover, the one she said she could never forget. The intensity of the loss fades with each passing day.

But life has the ability to surprise and shock. One evening, while entertaining a guest Eshei might have met just twice in her life, she offered a corner of her bed to him. He was too drunk to return to his hotel. He accepted the corner, but by daybreak they both were in each other's arms. In the morning half-light she cried and gave herself up to him. When she woke up, Eshei was a different woman. He prepared breakfast for her, and decided to stay with her. She was possessed by a new urge to betray, deceive her old lover. She was in full knowledge that her actions went against her principles and would traumatize a man she believed was in love with her. But she could not stop herself.

Ever so often, reality mocks the human need for equilibrium. The acts of destruction around her now offered clarity. She could rationalize why people did what they did. All she could was to write down her emotions to her lover: 'I have fallen to such lows, there's no way I can ever face you in my life. I have no intention of falling in love or having anything to do with him. I don't even know him. He happened to be around when I was feeling very lost, professionally and personally. What shall I do? I guess I never knew myself well enough. But I will never be morally, ethically right. I got off the moral high ground. That's the only thing I got out of whatever I did.There's so much to write, too much to tell you. But I am not capable of doing that. I might just hurt you more and more by saying what I want to. But someday I will definitely write to you. Today, everything is raw, too raw.'

Eshei would stare at the ceiling at night and clutch the corner of the bed and wonder where her life was leading her. Imprisoned by her demons, her nights were harassing her, interrogating her and she ran out of words, emotions and feelings.'I am sorry. I know that I have hurt you in the most horrendous way. You were all I wanted but I did the most horrible thing ever. I only regret what I have done. If you will give me a chance, I will try to give back whatever I took away.'

She remembered those times when extortion threats were made, her dad would be scared to take the call. Her own phone was now an instrument of torture for her. She would stare at the screen, waiting for a message and when the message arrived, she would shudder to read what it contained. 'I have developed some kind of a phobia. Since that incident happened, each time I see you calling, I wonder what the call will have in store for me ... my heart starts beating really fast, just like the time I got caught by my parents for doing things I was not supposed to do, that feeling where one knows that punishment is inevitable and no amount of escaping will help. But you just called to say you love me!'

At home, every evening people would go out and Eshei would ask them, 'Where are you going?' They would smile and say, 'Going to buy candles.' Eshei would wonder what was there to be happy about. 'But my happy Manipuri brother/sister will say, what can we do ... we have to buy candles since there is load-shedding every evening.' In her neighbourhood, 'going out to buy candles' was the time girls used to sneak out to meet their boyfriends and they would wait for load-shedding. 'So there was reason to be happy.'

But there was no happiness for her; she could not sleep at night.'I just lie there, watching the red glow of the mosquito repellent on the ceiling. I remember the innumerable times you put me on a pedestal, calling me morally upright, honourable, honest, pure ... these words have turned into a nightmare for me.'

'I have a morbid fear of sharp objects, especially razor blades, knives, sharp edges of a metallic can ... and all these words become sharp objects and cut me at night as

I look at the red glow. I imagine holding the word "pure" in my hand and it being taken away sharply, cutting my palm just as I've seen in old Hindi movies, a hero trying to hold a sword and as the sword was being pulled, the palm gets cut and those scenes would always make me flinch … I could never watch them … likewise, I can't watch my life now. Now I just want to meet you, see how much you cringe at the sight of me and then vanish for good.'

Eshei had lost all sense of how hurtful she was becoming. She went back on all her promises. She met her lover and found acceptance. But her lover's acceptance meant nothing and she was back to living her dual life. The same man was in her arms again. She betrayed him twice in a month and with the same person. She was caught again. This time, her lover embraced silence because nothing else was left to be said. He tried to accept the situation this time too but she had gone 'too far.' In her reverie, she even said that she had started wanting the other person. She said she was powerless to stop herself. She wanted to reclaim her youth. She was at her sadistic worst.

Is there going to be no response from you? Say it please. It will help ease the tension. Since the time I came in, I have not been able to do a single thing. Everywhere I am looking for a sign of you, why this silence suddenly?
Please say something.
I know I have no right asking anything from you. It's my selfishness going overboard.
But please allow me this one last time to be selfish.

Where are you? How are you?
Please write to me.

Eshei did not receive a single syllable. Death of a relationship was marked by silence and silence alone. Eshei had strange reasons for her loss of faith in her love as well as her homeland. She couldn't cut herself away from her own emotional bonds. She wanted a future with a past, without one jostling the other.

EIGHT

The Captain's Kitchen Garden

The reception was rather un-military. Instead of a suspicious jawan at the gate asking four and a half questions, an officer greeted us on this visit. There were tall glasses of tea and Good Day biscuits laid carefully on a tray. It was certainly not a permanent army base, where tea comes in standard cups accompanied with cocktail pakoras and samosas which have approved military sizes, like the length of the grass on the brigadier's office lawn. The base is actually a dilapidated cotton mill in the middle of a leikai. And like most public property in this valley, it has automatically passed on to the uniformed people.

The tea ceremony was observed in a room decorated with cheap China-made plastic flowers arranged in bottles of Old Monk. This was followed by a tour of the dormitory where weary soldiers were catching a nap that sometimes eludes them for days.

The landscape has an uncanny resemblance to a Vietnamese countryside during the American campaign, the backdrop of so many movies we have grown up with. Even the cane hats are similar and so are the faces under their shade with sandalwood paste to protect against sunburn.

Eighty-year-old Nga Gonomor believes that we've come with help to his village which has fallen off the map as far as government aid is concerned. Gonomor, a farmer in this Khurukul village tells us, 'There are a lot of problems, our dams do not work, the canals are broken, and there's hardly any money, please look into our situation.'

There are 10,000 farmers engaged in agriculture in this village. But for the Kharif crop, they don't get seeds supplied by the Ministry of Agriculture on time. This year the seeds arrived in May. For the Rabi crop, they have no water due to a shortage in the water storing facilities. They earn ₹80 a day during the season. A percentage of what they earn they must pay as tax to the militants. This fact is repetitive but for those who pay up, it's a reality they resent. And with farming turning rather unprofitable, young people are forced to look at other options and for some that meant taking up arms.

But this story is of the Captain Saab who took a break from his regular duties to accompany us to the paddy fields. In a faded white Maruti van, which was so useful under the circumstances, he ordered two of his finest men, dressed in plainclothes, to climb into the vehicle; they placed their guns under the seats.

We drove past two monitoring windows of the PLA, where some cadres must have made notes of our movements in tiny red notebooks. The road hasn't been repaired in the past decade or two. An overloaded Bedford city bus sways on both sides under its own weight; it is the only sound that rattles the countryside. The road ends at the magnificent Singha Dam, which at first sight, appears to be a rock-climbing destination.

It's a different matter that the dam has not been working for years and the area has gone without power for the last three days. When the power comes, it's only for a few hours. That's when all the households in Manipur get busy charging their electrical gadgets. Children switch on their games. Elders watch television. The son plugs in his electric guitar. It's a minor pandemonium. Every activity in the state is subject to power supply. The week is neatly divided into a flow chart. It is three days of ironing clothes, three days of Internet surfing. Mobile charging is often done through the vehicle battery and if the battery dies, nobody frets. Acceptance has been built into the psyche of the citizens.

Captain Saab was demonstrating his agility, holding a Kalashnikov against his chest and was running along the ledge of the dam when he spotted a group of men playing cards. He went up to them – they were sitting behind the powerhouse of the dam which was decorated with graffiti of one of the three dozen militant outfits that rule the state. The men were quick on their feet but the captain was quicker; he hugged the one who looked like a ringleader and whispered something in his ear. The ringleader's expression changed instantly and he invited us to tea. He was not in an encounter mode. Besides, the real ones are never encountered. The crash course instructed us to lie down and take cover of the vehicle if an encounter broke out.

The sky seemed more vast and darker than usual. That's because no construction broke the horizon for as long as the eye could see. It is the same sky over Myanmar and then China, which is not very far from where we were. Men and women in arched cane hats were ploughing a field, carrying concave rice baskets. One amongst them had a motor-run mini tractor which travelled up and down a small plot of land, making a noise that shattered an otherwise still landscape.

Captain Saab paused from time to time and congenially walked up to the farmers who seemed to know him. A familiar tension was growing but we knew that was induced by the area we were moving through. It was a hotbed of militant activity, even though it looked like a south-east Asian rice bowl. The men and women toiled to cultivate their produce, half of which would be handed over to the militants.

A cold wind blew in from somewhere across the valley. We were asked to wrap up as soon as we could. It was late afternoon and three soldiers were not enough to hold up an encounter. So we decided to retreat.The Maruti van raised as much dust as possible through the bloodied tracks of Singha and we entered the Rajput Rifles camp where a group of soldiers were having mugs of watered down dal and roti for a night they were not sure would pass uneventfully.

Light was failing. We had to travel another hour to enter a comparatively safer zone. And the Captain Saab's enthusiasm was contagious. He was about to unveil his greatest secret and we were led by a mini-parade to his kitchen garden. A military tarpaulin was pulled off in slow motion and what appeared was not exactly what we were expecting. A tractor. Yes, a blessed tractor, shining and waiting to get started! An emotional Captain Saab then related to us how he actually attended a college of agriculture, but after his friend died fighting in the Kargil war, he joined the short service commission of the army. Now he led a platoon that was occupying a cotton mill where 700 people were once employed. The Captain's sole ambition was to grow cotton in his kitchen garden and help the villagers reopen the cotton mill. Conflict throws up unsung heroes who more than often, depart silently.

The Captain has since been transferred and the cotton mill continues to host men in fatigues. The tractor has been auctioned. The beautiful countryside of Singha is still out of bounds. Stories of heroic efforts in Manipur are almost always swept away by the force of circumstances.

NINE

1989, 1995, 2009

I only have three photographs from my first visit to Manipur in 1989. A paddy field, a hut in the middle of nowhere and a bright sunset. These are not pictures which tell you the story of Manipur.

The 1989 photographs are very special and I carried them with me for years. The pictures say almost nothing, but it encapsulates a sense of deep foreboding. None of the pictures have any human form in the background or foreground. I cannot even recall the people I met during that visit. The places I visited are a permanent blur. I spent an entire day at a farm house in Kakching. I travelled to a hill where a Central Reserve Police Force (CRPF) convoy was ambushed a few days before we arrived. We were introduced to some young men running a mountaineering institute. We went to Moirang and made the ardous journey to Moreh. You already know how that turned out.

I purchased a silk wrap-around and a china tea set

from the market inside Burma. Women were selling pretty flowers along the roadside. Burma was a festering wound in the East, but for travellers like us, nothing appeared out of place.

I have a letter and a few poems from 1995. They're from a friend who is in a self-inflicted exile from Manipur. Those were letter writing days and he would carefully type out letters with addresses and dates, and use a whitener when required.

> *I've just returned from Imphal, in fact, and everything's dead there: hope, love, whathaveyou. The Meiteis are probably the most pretentious, shambolic, hypocritical people in the world. I'm enclosing a few new efforts of mine, just to let you know how I am feeling at the moment. The poems are not up to mark, derivative, and 'statemental.' But one must write to evade that deadline with death.*

While going through the letter, I found that the airfare between Guwahati and Imphal then was ₹470. Today it is ₹3000. The poet had invited me to attend his wedding, I couldn't attend. Exiled and wounded, he wrote about his adopted town:

> *Shillong is in a terrible shape at the moment. This missive should have reached you at least a week earlier but for the Khasi Students' Union who locked up the postal service, all government and educational institutions, banks, etc. during the whole of last week. Yes, given*

five years' time, this nervous hill-town, where all my youthful dreams were spawned, may no longer be a very salubrious place. It has given me a lot of love, of course, perhaps where none was deserved. But for how long can one live in exile? Remember Seferis' line: 'Wherever I travel Greece wounds me.' And frankly, I will not survive in a city for long. Even though I sometimes yearn for creature comforts, I'm still a provincial sonneteer at heart.

In another letter he wrote:

Having reached the crossroads of my life, my heart tells me to return to Manipur and do something useful there. I don't have faith in a liberated society but no one is going to impose a dress code, or a marriage code, or any code on me. Besides, I'm never going to give away my hard-earned cash to any half-baked revolution. I know I am inviting trouble, but it's too late to change now. I can never survive in an oppressive regime. That's why I didn't go back to Manipur.

His poems were powerful poems of love but in between the stanzas, the wounds of homelessness would cut deep into his thoughts:

This is the story of my people
We sowed suspicion in the fields
Hatred sprang and razed the crops
Now they go to gloating neighbours

Begging bowls in hand
Fingers pointed at each other
Their incessant bickering
Muffle all pity.
Our intentions are clear
Slash and burn,
Let fire erase all traces
So that suspicion cannot write our murderous history
Somewhere inside the labyrinth
We met, locked horns, and
Went our separate ways.
We believe our past is pristine
Even as we reaped heads and took slaves
When we rewrite make-believe history
With malicious intent,
Memory burns on a short fuse.

In an almost violent denial of what these poems say was Eshei's insistence that home is finally in Manipur: 'I might stay anywhere, do anything, but it will be with Manipur in my heart. I can't forget the first time I returned and what I felt for the place in 2005. The last three years gave me an understanding of the place I used to call my state. Do I sound like a patriot? Doesn't really matter how I sound. And I KNOW that I cannot change Manipur's fate, BUT that does not mean I will not try. There are so many things I can't change.' Eshei's outburst was mostly out of exasperation and not conviction. But homecoming is a journey a lot of people in this region have never experienced.

Assam was part of undivided Bengal prior to the establishment of Chief Commissioner's Province in 1912. After Partition, millions of people scampered across to India, to be stamped forever as refugees. Most of them were Bengali Hindus who left their land and property and came across overnight. There was another relocation of Bengali Muslims which later transformed into a continuous flow of migrants – even after the formation of Bangladesh. Assam and Bengal had to bear the burden of the immigrant population and this became the platform on which Assam politics is staged to this day.

For those millions of people and the next generation, the concept of 'home' was reduced to just a house. At various phases, these people were either ousted from their addresses or displaced from their adopted home. It was not only the migration from East Bengal, but a very large population travelled from Bihar and Nepal and constituted the region's labour force. With time, this force was replaced by yet another influx of 'aliens', as illegal migration from Bangladesh continued unabated. This migration changed demographies and created a new socio-political landscape.

But for many like Eshei who ethnically belonged to the region, homecoming had assumed a different meaning altogether. They were forced to seek occupation outside the region, and knew very well that it might never be possible to return.

A year later, Eshei who had already moved out of the state, looked back at the 'homecoming' and recollected:

'Last time when I was home, I felt that going back home was no longer about being with my family, having home-cooked food and get-togethers. It was about confronting so many things that I feel I was running away from. Everything was the same; nothing moved – only I was moving, rest was static. I felt ashamed too, thinking about how I am constantly escaping. But from what?' The confrontation was easy. But nothing followed. It was always a dead end.

I had almost forgotten my first visit to Manipur. I hadn't met the people I would never forget. I had no recollection of the girls. I just remember them zipping past in their two-wheelers through congested alleys. The poems my friend would send, conveyed to me a sense of the place, but it never prepared me for the tumultuous decade I spent discovering its underbelly.

TEN

Journey

It was meant to be a short journey which became the most memorable travel experience. It was very visual and not the kind that can be captured well in words.

Manipur was burning. It was not a Naga-Meitei clash but on the surface it might have appeared to be so. Manipur has hills surrounding the valley where the majority of the population live and where the shredded economy thrives.

The valley has the Meiteis and the hills are sparsely filled with a number of tribes, many are politically identified as Nagas and Kukis although culturally they are different and exist in the census record as individual tribes. There is no recorded date of their claim, but it is now an established nomenclature, although not one that has been ratified by the Indian Constitution. One such tribe is the Thangkul tribe who prefer to be identified as Nagas.

From my childhood, I remember a tall Thangkul student who would bring home baskets of small red apples. I never knew that he came from such an interesting land.

In the 1960s, one such student from the hills of Manipur joined the Naga insurgency and then brutally overran his rival, a Hemi Naga from Myanmar, and established the supremacy of his faction of Naga insurgents. He was a Thangkul and a student of St Anthony's College in Shillong. He took the fight right to the Indian government with considerable success. He also spread terror across the region and helped create the industry of insurgency.

Our journey was to the village of this terrorist leader, but he was never called a terrorist. He was the leader of the 'great Naga cause', a separatist leader fighting for Naga Unity (by indulging in fratricide, extortion, abduction and every conceivable terrorizing activity).

How did the Thangkul from Manipur, whose ancestors' history was interlinked with Manipur, become a Naga – it is not known. But that's another story which has two versions: The Naga story and the Meitei claim.

Now in the midst of this serious violence, I met two young men who came down from Delhi and were eager to guide me past the smoke screen to the 'real place.' In a 'still working condition' jeep, we left for Ukhrul town. The journey as far as I can remember, was peaceful and good and the great speeches made by the two men on the 'Naga cause' were enough to keep me engaged. Suddenly, there was calm after the incessant clamour of protests in the valley.

But stories can also break calm. Especially when they

convey threat or fear. The men parked the jeep at a bend. It was very quiet. Then they climbed a hillock and pulled me there as well to demonstrate how their comrades ambushed an army convoy going up to Ukhrul to take their positions. Twenty army men were killed in the infamous Ukrul ambush. That night when the convoy arrived in Ukhrul, it was a night of death and drunkenness, with the army men lusting for revenge.

Ukhrul presented itself as a 'nothing-really-happened' town. We were dropped near the deputy commissioner's office, adjoining a large field. The guides directed my gaze to a hill range behind, showing me the famous Shiroi hill where the stunningly beautiful Shiroi lily is found. This flower doesn't grow anywhere else in the world. This name has been used in numerous movies, restaurants, homes, and hotels of Manipur. Shiroi is probably one Naga word that the Meitei may want to claim as their own, considering how popular it is in the valley. The Meitei will however challenge this by saying that Shiroi belongs to them. I have not seen the lily which people there refer to as 'shirui.' This is one place I have missed travelling to. The lily blooms in Shirui kashong, named after a mythical queen Shirui Philava who is believed to reside there. So if one can manage to see the lily it would probably be like meeting the queen.

Ukhrul doesn't have decent accommodation and the only one available was a broken-down shack run by a young Sikh man with very typical Thangkul features. A little incongruous in that landscape, but it's not difficult to guess where he came from: a routine case of an army man who must have been posted in Manipur and fell in love with a local girl. In fact, Major H St P Maxwell, who became the political agent immediately after the Anglo-Manipur war of 1891, had also married a local girl. The 'local' girl was no ordinary lady, but a Manipuri princess. She was the daughter of Maharaja Sur Chandra, who came to the throne in 1886 after the death of his illustrious father, Maharaja Chandrakirti. He ruled till 1891, when he was dethroned by his half-brother, Maharaja Kullachandra. The fight between these two Majarajas led to the British interference and the Anglo-Manipur war of 1891, after which the British annexed Manipur and its government came directly under the British crown.

By dinner time, the ambience had changed. I was sandwiched between two warring Thangkul cousins arguing over a steaming dinner of cabbage leaves, un-skinned dry chicken, rice and a really hot pickle which could very well be one cause of their violent streak. The argument had nothing to do with food and concentrated on whether I should be guided the next morning to Somdel, the village of the dreaded terrorist leader.

The night passed in the decrepit motel. Even the door wouldn't bolt. It was July but the night was chilly. The next morning the cousins didn't arrive, so I knew they had decided to abandon me. Now the Thangkul Sikh was our only hope of arranging a vehicle to Somdel. No vehicle was willing to take us there, so we had almost written off Ukhrul with dejection and disappointment.

The cousins finally arrived in their jeep and we set off to the village. The first roadblock was slush; the jeep manoeuvered with great difficulty. The road was lost into a dirt track and by then we had lost all hope of reaching Somdel. The vehicle was slowly zigzagging when we caught sight of a few church spires in the horizon. Somdel was close.

When we actually reached the village gate, it was difficult to imagine that a village such as Somdel existed. It was beautiful, as though the world had almost ended. Men and women received us and paraded children dressed in their traditional best to welcome the first-ever television crew to the Muivah and Shimrey households.

Concrete houses and massive churches. How did they ever carry so much building material and so far! The first sight was significant. The terrorist leader's brother was planting a white flag of reconciliation on his rooftop. Then the village choir sang for us. After that we were served a large breakfast of cakes and boiled eggs with mugs of tea. Strangely, I have very little recollection of the conversation we had. But the 'unique Naga history' was not fed to me there. It seemed to me that there was a sense of resignation as well as hope for reconciliation.

They also presented us with beautiful woven shawls. Their 'Naganess' is probably apparent in their designs. The colour combination is very sophisticated. The Naga shawls are undoubtedly the north-east's best design export and competes closely with Assam's muga silk mekhela chador, saris, scarves, drapes and they are still discovering more ways of popularizing the fabric. It took me several years before I knew where this bright colour in Naga textiles came from. A French lady who works closely with textiles recently informed me that the 'Naga red' is a term used even in Europe because that is the reddest of the red used in textiles. The red comes from the root of a plant called Madder or Rubia Sikkimensis. Sometimes they also add the essence of other plants.

Somdel had been conquered. There was not a hint of any Naga insurgency there. It was a near-sovereign land and the people seemed happy and peaceful. There were no gun-toting Naga soldiers or Indian Army soldiers. Nobody spoke of insurgency and even less of the man they either revered or feared.

We returned, but not before the jeep broke down midway. In an age and place where cellphones had not found their way as yet, we had to send a messenger back to the village for a spare jeep. A WWII Willy carried us across the treacherous hills and back to the streets of Ukhrul, where a giant rally was awaiting our participation.

ELEVEN

Catch Them Young

At the other end of the valley in Kuki-dominated Churachandpur, a group of very young boys show how they have been campaigning against drugs. They beat a middle-aged man who they alleged was peddling pharmaceutical drugs. The man fell on his feet and begged forgiveness. A teenaged boy took out a shining pistol and shot him in his left knee. They might have sent the man back home or killed him. Vigilante justice is routine amongst the terrorist outfits that control Manipur. And this detail about shooting knees is a popular form of 'punishment.' Eshei or any of her friends who are so enlightened about the history of their race and the culture of their people were not exposed to these hills. Imphal was not oblivious to these incidents but preferred to ignore the mutinies that were being acted out.

Done with the job at hand, the boy goes back to being a youngster. Outside the room with the corrugated roof where the man was shot, a group of teenagers were playing a game of carrom. The eldest had a gun tucked under his belt. That's a constant reminder of their other life.

Thirteen-year-old Brandy is the darling of the group. He is the youngest and has been nominated as their spokesperson because he knows a little bit of English. But he hardly has any thoughts to communicate. He and his friends are the terrorists' most powerful weapon along the Indo-Myanmar border. Young. Enthusiastic. Fearless. Impressionable. They come cheap, eat less, travel light and are easy to manipulate. And they have very few demands.

Brandy speaks: 'I can't remember when I joined. I went to school in Mizoram, till class six. I miss my friends and family but I enjoy life with the guerillas. We do anything that we are ordered to do. I'm not afraid of guns, although I haven't killed anyone yet. But if any member from my family or friends opposes our group, I will surely kill him.'

That's pretty much what all the boys say. They will kill anyone their commander asks them to.

Moirou joined the underground in 2005, believing that 'my land and people need me, I never went back to my home since I joined. I've killed three persons so far in encounters, I've got experience of other encounters as well.'

Seventeen-year-old Moirou is one of the hundreds of children recruited by militant outfits here. Hundreds of young boys and girls pick up the gun when they should be going to school. The boys demonstrate their combat skills. The smallest boys are placed closest to the enemy, because their leaders say they are the most fearless. And when they are not feeling so brave, they are given helpful doses of drugs.

Siamthianmuan has 'never been afraid of the gun ... I don't miss my family ... I chose to be a militant.' The pride is evident. However, the cause is unknown, even to him.

According to United Nations, there are an estimated 2,50,000 child soldiers around the world. Every year the number grows, as more children are recruited for use in active combat. But Moirou and his friends are not accounted in this data.

Other outfits don't recruit but outsource teenagers to ferry explosives, lob grenades. Sometimes they get blown up because they are not properly trained. Akon blew up a railway colony market in Guwahati with an auto-van carrying gas cylinders for home delivery. He said 'Moi bhalkoi chaw chaw kham.' All he wanted in exchange for this act was a good Chinese meal at a city restaurant. In another incident, two young men were given cellphones in exchange for carrying explosives and planting it on the route of the then-Foreign Minister's visit.

There are some who can't handle the life as an underground operative. Food is scarce. The treks through jungles are tough and malaria stalks these cadres every day. Muang joined up when she was fifteen. At nineteen, she's a young mother who has recently quit the force. 'I joined in 2003; that life was difficult at times. I've never killed anyone. If girls want to marry, they are allowed to quit. I had joined the outfit because I was interested in the war.'

Girls are particularly at risk of rape and abuse. Still several outfits find them useful.

Some of the boys carry photographs of their girlfriends from back home. They hope to return someday. Many of them attended school, but then they were convinced that the gun was a better tool against a society they perceived had only abused them.

The more familiar face of a child soldier is from Sierra Leone, Uganda or Rwanda or even closer home in Afghanistan, but there is hardly any international or national concern about the hundreds of children recruited, trained, maimed, and killed in conflicts in India – particulary in the north-east. The use of children as soldiers has been universally condemned as abhorrent and unacceptable. Yet very little has been done to address this issue. Has the Indian government raised this issue with the NSCN-IM, a group they have been in a ceasefire agreement for years and which is known to recruit children? Child abuse has never been on the mind of any policy maker in this country.

From Ukhrul to Churachandpur to Tamenglong, wherever one travelled to, militant assertions by tribes and communities played out with a vengeance. But in the midst of the mindless violence, stories of courage and hope brought people from opposite ends together, creating bonds that would last a lifetime.

TWELVE

The Village

'But how did you get away? I was sure I shot you right in the chest. Let's see?'

A diminutive man wearing an oversized shirt and farmer's trousers raised himself slightly on his toes to take a long look. D unbuttoned his shirt and said, 'You were sharp, but something came in between.' It was a crucifix his father had brought back as a memento from a visit to Rome in 1962; incidentally he was wearing it on that day. The right arm of the crucifix is broken, but he has never taken it off since that night. He rolled up his sleeves and displayed the scar. 'This is where the bullet finally hit me.'

D has been reliving the incident for the past sixteen years, but he was not prepared for this particular encounter. It was surreal. 'Thank God we are alive; we came so close to killing each other.'

It was a sultry night in 1996. But an entire village stayed up. Each time a twig cracked in the woods, they felt it was the enemy arriving. When they finally arrived, it was past two in the morning. Both were taken by surprise.

It took D hours to cross the Barak River and approach the Upper Longdipabram village. 'Longdipabram was not my original destination. It was near Theron, the area where there are multi-layered caves and a Kuki village. I was there to protect them from an attack. I went there from Molsang village to Longdipabram and I reached at about three in the morning. It was a five-hour walk.' Even today, it takes an hour on foot to reach there after a tough trek from the main township. D had no idea that the villagers were on vigil that night. The village chief was atop a tree watchtower till midnight. He had gone to catch some sleep when the men arrived.

All afternoon, Atenbo and his villagers were trying to persuade four Naga terrorists to flee. They had come to the village to collect punishment tax after the villagers had stolen pigs and set fire to a neighbouring Kuki village. The Kukis and Nagas were caught in a deadly fight in the hills of Manipur.

These tribal denominations can be confusing. This is a Zeliangrong village but they have been under diktat to align with the NSCN-IM. This is part of a larger design by the leader of a terrorist group to integrate tribal-dominated districts of the neighbouring states of Nagaland into what he calls Greater Nagaland or Nagalim for Christ.

Atenbo, the Zeliangrong village chief, failed to make any breakthrough with the armed tax collectors when he asked them to vacate the village. The gunmen refused to leave. Atenbo knew the consequences. The men in uniform arrived and cordoned the village. The chief knew they were coming and directed the men to the house where the four gunmen were waiting. He had no option.

A sudden shot scattered the men and the early morning quiet was shattered with a fierce exchange of fire. These forests were familiar with the sound of gunfire, but this was war.

D's carbine stopped working. He continued fighting. A bullet hit him below his waist. The door of the house flew out towards him and as he dodged the flying piece of wood another bullet hit him somewhere near the chest.

A grenade was hurled at Atenbo and his right foot bore the brunt of the blast. D was thrown on the ground but not before he took one of the gunmen down with him. One escaped and two were caught. D was bleeding profusely and needed help. In a swift evacuation operation, the helicopter arrived but he wouldn't leave till a six-year-old boy and a thirteen-year-old girl were rescued before him. The pilot had strict instructions to carry him, but D wanted the children to be evacuated first.

Atenbo recounted that while he held D's bleeding body, a radio message arrived, probably from the senior officers. The message in Hindi clearly said that the villagers should be annihilated. Kill all. Those days when media did not quite exist, entire villages would disappear. Human rights wasn't in vogue.

D reacted and used his dying wish as a strategy. 'No one should be hurt, sir. Not till I am alive.' A furious platoon with their officer near death were in no mood to let anybody get away. They brought the two gunmen and waited for orders to torture and shoot them. D refused to comply with their wishes.

Atenbo broke down as he started narrating that night's story. The small playground of Longdipabram was suddenly the stage for a poignant drama. His right leg is now slightly stretched but unless he mentions it, a casual observation may not reveal any discomfort. The nagging ache from reconstructive surgery is not visible on his face. Long years of living with it has eased the pain and trauma.

Those were fierce fighting years. Sixteen years ago, as a convoy of the Indian army moved up to take position, aircrafts would fly ahead clearing ambushes. As soon D's company reached the destination, he went on a week's leave. When he returned, it had nearly been a month. So he was sent on a punishment patrol in the jungles of Tamenglong when he was faced with this encounter.

At first sight, the village appears to be a bit of an error in judgment. The road across a few hills and streams and a river are picture-postcard pretty but it makes no sense to have come this far to find nothing and then set up a village. Why did Atenbo's forefathers come so far? They surely weren't born here. They migrated.

All that the young captain carried was a map and the crucifix pendant from the Vatican that his father had brought back to his Baptist village. A cross that decided his life and the fate of the villagers. One that he must carry all his life.

A mother remembered the cross. She took it in her

hand and wailed inconsolably. She had brought a basket of oranges for the officer who saved the lives of her children. They would have died that day, if D hadn't insisted on their evacuation before his own rescue.

Tears are contagious. Under the unusually warm spring sun, an entire congregation stood in tears. Many had no recollection of that night. Some remembered every beat of the silence that came in between the radio messages of a captain and his officer. The captain chose to defy orders. A village was saved.

The road to Tamenglong town was winding but surprisingly motorable. In sharp contrast to most of the state's roadways, this road was like a garden path leading you to a picturesque hill town. And here was a town standing at crossroads with its bloodied past and a passive present. As D entered the town, a mela with its Ferris wheels and motorbike daredevils were entertaining the people. Children gunned down colourful balloons to win packets of biscuits, hooplas for soap bars and a bottle of Old Monk rum as the jackpot. Urban India has now adopted other forms of entertainment, so melas and circuses survive in towns like this one.

Colonel Saab's officers' mess was a large room with chandeliers, where uniformed jawans were on a mission to get their guests drunk. Pakoras, cashewnuts, tikkas made their rounds without pausing. A military band played in the lawns.

For the first time since D landed at the airport, a man who accompanied the village chief started talking.

He was soft and gentle. He recounted every event since the evacuation. It was his son who was injured, along with his sister. They managed to reach Tamenglong, but they had to be rushed to Imphal. That was not easy. At Imphal, the hospital staff did not attend to the patients for a long time.

Time had passed. His sister was married off to a much older but affluent man. His son was studying. But both required a good diet and regular medical attention. He worked as much as he could to meet the medical expenses. His voice faltered and in the large military atmosphere everyone listened to his story without any interruption. Even the tikkas slowed down. In a room filled with war memorabilia, none of the spoils of war proudly sitting on the tables seemed to understand the futility of it all. For sixteen long years, this man had been toiling to bring up a handsome young boy whose head aches intermittently and sometimes, his memory fails him. But his community is glad that he is alive. The memories of that one night have become a lifetime of anecdotes.

The young boy could not stop crying as he held D tightly. The girl sitting next to him was also without any emotion. A teardrop steadied itself on her transfixed eyes for a long time before it coursed down her face. When her mother held D's face, the daughter cried. That moment of intense pain returned with an inexplicable emotion. Here was a man who had saved her. They did not know what happened to each other. But somewhere in their memory, that moment of agony was still alive. Even though he was bleeding profusely, D tried to calm her with some sweets he found in his pockets. She withdrew. Later in the hospital bed D would write in his diary:

> *I looked at the girl. She was very young perhaps six or seven. Her body was trembling. Her eyes are red, so are her hands. It is her blood let out by bullets that pierced through her tender hands. The little girl's pain and tears hurt me more than my own wounds.*
>
> *I try to turn over to touch the girl to wipe her tears. Her fear and possibly the pain increases. I try to give her a chocolate. She doesn't take it. Perhaps she has never seen one or she doesn't want it from me. I try smiling. She is confused. I cannot believe how close she came to dying. An innocent angel. Only chance spared her then. Yet she had no chance of survival if she didn't reach a hospital soon enough. The nearest hospital was at Tamenglong District which was six hours away on foot. Perhaps that may be too late.*
>
> *The chopper arrived to take me to the military hospital. I requested for the girl to be evacuated to Tamenglong where my battalion was stationed. The pilot refused, insisting that I needed immediate medical attention and doubted if he could even reach me in time. I spoke to my commanding officer Colonel Vipin Nautiyal and requested him that if need be consider it as my last wish. The girl left for Tamenglong.*
>
> *I knew her death would neither be illegal nor immoral. It would have been reported as 'killed or*

injured in crossfire.' But I knew I couldn't carry the burden of guilt of the death of an innocent child who didn't even know the name of the region or even the village that lay beyond her wooden home nor her religion – in whose names we were fighting in her courtyard.

Uniformed men were hated in these parts. They are still not welcome. But there are some stories of hope and faith that remain unforgettable for both the storyteller as well as the listener.

THIRTEEN

Punish the Tiger

Like imagined homelands, contested identities and revivalists, Manipur too has a rich tradition of folktales.

'At last the young ones of the village will be able to see and witness in actualities. It was done way back in the year 1974 at Sungkuang. Afterwards, it was not conducted anymore and this ritual performance is possible only when Khuplianthang, the hunter, catches the tiger. Now we will showcase it, physically. It is a sign of victory over others and is a must-do as per our custom. This is a mark of our edge over others as men. According to our folktales, in the days of yore, human and beast lived together in harmony and took a vow not to disturb each other.'

'But as the beasts have violated the terms of agreement, so man must overpower them. Now we are performing this to show our prowess over the beasts and to punish them. This is to show the animal's disloyalty and violation of the terms of our agreement. This is the latest performance and is being performed at Zokhonuam (village) today, 21 April 2010. And as I have said before, since time immemorial when man and beast lived together in harmony, an agreement was made with the beast, but the tigers have violated those terms. This shows our power over the tiger.'

'As per our long-held beliefs, if this ritual is not performed, after we die we violate our terms with the tigers and its spirits. So the tiger will eat our flesh and bones, eyes, ears, nose, and other parts of our body, by digging it out from our graveyards. This could really happen and the tiger will eat our corpses and particularly our fingers, nose, nails. We perform this ritual to protect ourselves from that eventuality.'

Zenith, with woollen floral headgear and feathers, came across as someone younger than a village headman, but this is something that he has inherited. Not the headgear, the designation.

As Thuang narrated the tradition of killing tigers to Eshei, people were dancing around the bonfire while women were serving rice beer. It took the village sixteen days of preparation for this ritual. Eshei was struck by the way the headman narrated the story. Folktales as Eshei knew always started with 'a long time ago there once lived'and so on. This was real. It wasn't in the realm of fantasy.

The ritual was almost over but a 'pacification ceremony' had yet to be performed. An old man uttered a sentence like a testament and said: 'Now you are under my feet due to your insincerity,' and he stepped on the tiger's dead body.

Then another said, 'You are a liar, defaulting on your promises and vows to us. I jump over you here.' That was followed by gunshots and dances that lasted the whole night. Men and women held hands and danced under the moonlight.

When Eshei reached the village after a day's trek through leech-infested forests, the preparation for the ritual was almost over. The cow had been slaughtered and two large pots of rice beer were placed in the middle of the ritual ground. The tiger, which in this case was actually a clouded leopard, was hanging upside down with all its limbs tied to a bamboo and supported by two poles. People came to those pots and sucked a little beer through a bamboo nipple and spat out the liquid.

Wild boar was being cooked nearby; some were testing the two-inch bamboo flutes while another was trying out the lugubrious ancestral drum. Metal gongs were played to maintain the beat, and muskets which were used in earlier hunts were being cleaned to witness the superiority of man over beast.

Five elderly men sat around the muskets and narrated the significance of the ritual to Eshei again: 'When our forefathers caught tigers from the forest, they were first kept in the forest near the village, they were barred from entering the village. This was done because the tigers are large wild beasts. A ritual ceremony has to be performed first. If that is not done, after we die, the tiger spirit and or any other tiger will scavenge the hunter's corpse and devour the eyes, ears, nose, hands and legs. Therefore, a reception ceremony is a must. Through the rituals we attribute blame upon the tiger for violating the terms and agreements made with the tigers by man and other animals, in the remote past when they lived together in harmony. We warn it not to step into our cottages and our land. We study the fault of the tiger. If it was killed, a reception ceremony is usually conducted near the village by blowing flutes, beating drums. In the evening after all birds and animals hastened back to their nests and homes, the evening ceremony is held for the tiger's soul and to signify that the tigers are blameworthy.'

Then they sing, 'Your own worthlessness has caused you to die.' Another villager adds, 'If we don't perform the rituals, we are violating our traditional practices and have to bear all the consequences.' The group of dancers then danced one by one, crouching slightly and matching their steps with the drum and gong.

The hunt which Eshei missed was reconstructed by enthusiastic hunters. The forest adjoining the village near the stream is where the cat had marked its territory. Khupliangthang followed it and shot it just near the cave which was its home. Then, as the hunter arrived near the village called Khomual with his prize catch, he gave a victory cry called 'Hanla' which signals the villagers of his arrival. Others fired their gun, 'Mualsah,' informing that all hunters have returned. The villagers then trouped in to welcome the hunters.

At Khomual they celebrated and danced to gunshots to mark their victory, with women presenting flowers to their male counterparts. They danced holding the heads of previous tigers killed in the village.

Eshei's bookshop partner was slowly moving out. Her roommate was also leaving. The business was floundering. It was then that she decided to start writing. Folktales have been written and rewritten. Eshei was excited about the huge scope of documenting oral literatures. The clouded leopard would be her first.

When Eshei returned to the lights and the noise from this almost make-believe experience, she had a long mail waiting for her. The tiger seemed to be on her trail.

FOURTEEN

Total Recall, Tiger and I

1990s. After a quiet day out in the forest, I return to my very pretty but rugged room-with-an-attic and stare at the wall before me. People are atop jeeps and elephants, looking through their binoculars for who else, the tiger. And behind a reasonably faraway thick patch of a vantage point in the same frame, the tiger mans the route of these 'wild visitors', with his own pair of binoculars. The blurb might as well have said, never the twain shall meet. This well-framed sketch of a typical 'wildlifing' moment in my forest lodge leaves me with two thoughts – who is watching whom? and of the political possibilities of wildlife cartoons. The moment would have continued to remain sort of snigger-split-second funny, had it not been followed by gunshots in the distance.

Flashback to the Nigerian countryside, 1979-1982.

As a kid studying in Mussoorie, with parents posted in Nigeria, it was what I now call the Post-Age. Doubly thrilling because letters from home meant I would have more 'junglee stamps' to add to what just might have been the chief hobby of the post-age generation. These Nigerian stamps were green and always had one of the big cats. Usually a cheetah or an African leopard. And taking long train trips while on holiday in Africa in that particularly-fun-for-kids-railway specialty – the saloon, I saw my stamps come alive before me. In the wild.

And it is somewhere there that I recall being told, 'You guys are lucky in India, you have the tiger and the lion. The only country in the world to have both.' I would go in all my educated ignorance – 'Really?' (It's a fact I will be reminded of again, when I briefly work as a freelance wildlife tour escort in India, but that is in late 90s).

The letter was from a friend she went to college with. Eshei was hungry but there was nothing to eat. The trek back was tiring and though tiger meat and wild boar was available, she preferred mashed potatoes and cabbage leaves with a strange smelling rice.

Now she wanted something urban. This town had none of it. Till recently, the only restaurant was a shabby 'rice hotel' or 'chak cha hotel' at the bus depot. Suddenly Fat James with his Thai and Chinese cuisine arrived in Churachandpur – this was the first sign of change in the battered town Eshei would spend the night in.

Eshei continued reading the letter.

Mid to-end 1990s – I roam India with a friend who has a more instinctive connection with animals. We loaf away the country sides. Walking with some forest guards in I can't even remember where all, who teach me how first-person stories are first the personal memorabilia of an instinct, sharpening with each experience in the wild. While being unputdownable, these are not always found only in books. Other much-recalled instances of pride of the old forest officer lot in knowing their wildlife, hunter turning into conservationist – moments that not a zillion bonfire sessions made stale. Mountain wildernesses in a range of seasons, and of course us, travelling for no ostensible reason. India, in each geographical speck when left alone, was torridly inviting. And we'd invited ourselves. Was I only being prepared for my first 'adult' beastly moment?

Eshei's connection with animals was just about leaving them alone. But a good listener in a forest helps. Even the beast respects silence.

The friend's letter just brought back the jungle treks into her hungry night. Fat James had shut shop and there was nothing else available. No one here ventures out at night. Eshei was familiar with the nights in Manipur. Familiarity and acceptance though, are different. The tension of what may happen next was almost similar to the forests at night.

A jungle could connect to what was wild in the human. This genetic coding-decoding of an evolutionary rhythm was felt, in the famous words of a Madonna song – 'Touched for the very first time.' This humility, of feeling like you're just one species out there with many before you. And that taut, on-your-guard awareness of just being there.

So this, that and the other were interconnecting for Eshei, like a mad song you half remember, off a breaking radio-wave. And one that you couldn't stop humming if you tried.

That night, the only connection she could make was a beastly hunger for food. In moments of vulnerability, reason often gives away to the subconscious urges. Eshei wanted someone to talk to. Someone who would take care of her. In the most unexpected moments, life's fancies ambushed her. Like the 'ambushes' she has heard so much about. In a conflict zone, the vocabulary is punctuated with violent thoughts. Eshei recalls being told how the guerillas generally prefer some source of water at ambush points. It takes a long time to select a place and lie in ambush for an even longer time. That is why the water source is important. Water source is also important for setting up camps and during an operation, the security forces would try and choke the enemy's water sources and then the food supply.

If one drives through the tribal areas of Manipur and Nagaland, the most common sight is of a shabbily dressed man with a gun. Even though there maybe nothing left to hunt, the hunter patiently spends all day looking for a catch and is satisfied if he can bring home a bird.

It's worse in Nagaland. Birds hardly chirp, and animals are never on the prowl. The local markets display a variety of animals on sale: monkeys, flying squirrels, deer, bear and birds. But such markets are soon going to be selling chicken instead of their exotic collection of endangered wildlife. Where is the wildlife?

When she turned the pages of the retold folktales of Nagaland that were sent to her by a friend, she came across tales and sketches of tigers. It surprised her. It's difficult to spot a dog in that state, so where did the tiger come from?

In her childhood, the tiger folktale that was narrated was of the Tapta. 'A long time ago,' as it began in any folktale, in any part of the world – there was once a man and his wife in a village in Manipur. The couple did not have a child for a long time. Finally, after lots of offering to the gods, a son was born to them. The child was rather stubborn. Once he started crying to get his demands and wishes, he wouldn't stop until he got it. So the couple would take turns to take care of their troublesome son. It was Wednesday. The night was engulfed under a cover of darkness. It was pouring. In the stable outside, a tiger was hiding to attack the horse in the stable. At the same time, a thief was also lurking in the dark to steal the horse from that very stable which was located in the front yard of the house.

Unable to pacify the crying child inside the house, the man stepped out on the portico of his house. The child was still crying. The man made yet another attempt to stop the ceaseless crying by threatening him with the imminent arrival of a tiger. To stop the boy's crying, the man looked at his son and said, 'Hey look, the tiger is coming, the tiger is coming.' The very words used by the father to his son made the tiger outside panic. The tiger thought that the man had seen him. So the animal did his best to hide from the man. But the child continued crying.

The wife was on her way back home, and to protect herself from the rain, she used a yenpak, a wide hat made of bamboo shoot fly sheets. In order to take her by surprise, the man in a loud voice said, 'Oh! My god, here comes Tapta, here comes Tapta.' On hearing 'Here comes Tapta', the child trembled with fear and stopped his crying. The son embraced his father. Sensing the fear in his child now he said, 'Go back Tapta, and go back Tapta to your place. My son has stopped crying.'

As the mother stood motionless, the four-legged animal thought that the shadowy motionless figure at the edge of the portico was that of Tapta. Both the thief and tiger were scared. The name of Tapta got the child to stop his endless crying, so they thought that the Tapta was a strong, ferocious and intelligent animal.

The tiger fearfully approached the horse and paused. Meanwhile the thief moved slowly to mount the horse so as to run away on horseback. In the dark, the man was searching for the horse. Incidentally, he touched one of the legs of the tiger. When the thief touched his leg, the tiger thought that the ferocious Tapta had touched him. The great animal was coming to kill him. He was so frightened that he would grant Tapta a ride on his back. On the other hand, the thief also thought that a horse with large legs was faster than one with thin and small legs. So he searched out the large and heavy legs of the tiger. Thinking that it was a good horse, he mounted the animal. The tiger followed the man's commands. The tiger was in fear of Tapta. He thought that he would become a prey of Tapta if he opposed the commands.

The tiger was running here and there in abandon. The man thought he was riding a short-legged horse. As the tiger was running as fast as he could to save his life, he didn't look to see who was riding on his back. The man also didn't look to see what kind of animal he was riding. In the darkness they did not see each other. It was still raining. They ran till dawn. At last, the man knew that he was riding on the back of a tiger. He grew fearful. But he planned to alight from the running tiger. Suddenly, the man jumped off the back of the running tiger and his hand grasped a branch of the tree that was growing on the roadside. He was hanging on to the branch. But the tiger was running faster without looking behind. The tiger ran past bushes and jungles, and at long last, he met a bear. The bear halted the tiger and said, 'Ah! My friend, where are you running off to in such speed?' The tiger, panting, replied, 'Oh my god, I am very fortunate to escape the clutches of Tapta.' Saying this, the tiger again tried to run. But the bear stopped his friend and pacified him. The bear asked, 'Who is Tapta? What about his physical structure? Where is he?'

With fear writ large on his face, the tiger said, 'The dreaded Tapta was on the branches of the tree. He was hanging from the branches.' Saying this, the tiger pointed his right paw to the mango tree growing in the distance. The bear suggested, 'Come on, let us go there and kill that wild and ferocious beast.' But the tiger rejected the suggestion and said, 'I am afraid of Tapta, if you want to go there, you go alone and kill him.' The tiger ran as fast as he could. While running he shouted, 'Here comes the dreaded Tapta, here comes the mighty Tapta.'

The bear came to the spot where the tiger had pointed his finger. The man hid himself in a hole at the base of the tree.The bear looked up at the tree. He did not find any object. So again he searched for Tapta in the hole. The bear pushed his tiny tail into the narrow hole. Fearing his life, the man held the tail using all his strength and suddenly released it. The bear was thrown on the ground. Now the bear freaked out; he got up and started running, saying, 'No Tapta, no Tapta, it is the tail puller, the tail puller.' While running for his life, the bear met an elephant on his way. He was stopped by the elephant who asked, 'Oh my friend, what had happened? Can I help you?' Pointing his finger to the tree, the bear said, 'A tail puller is hiding inside the hole of that dead tree.'

Surprised, the elephant suggested his friend to go together to examine the tree. The bear refused and said, 'You go alone, I am afraid of the tail puller.' The elephant said, 'If you fear, you sit on my back and let us go there and see it.' The bear was relieved when he heard the courageous suggestion given by his friend. Sitting on the back of the elephant, the bear came towards the spot. The largest land animal with its long trunk hanging down from its head to the ground, started smelling the hole of the dead tree. Inside the hole, the man panicked and dragging out his small knife, cut a small piece of the elephant's trunk. Traumatized, the elephant pulled out his trunk and ran as fast as he could, shouting, 'No tail puller, no tail puller, it is trunk cutter, the trunk cutter.'

While running towards the den of the lion, the elephant said it was trunk cutter, but the bear sitting on the elephant's back said it was tail puller. Their argument continued till they arrived at the lion's den. Upon reaching the den, they had seen that the tiger had already taken his seat near the lion. Approaching the lion, the two terrified animals saw that the tiger was narrating his story about a ferocious beast called Tapta. The bear added to the story and said that the beast was tail puller. The elephant said that the beast was no ordinary animal; it was indeed the trunk cutter. The king of the beasts was in a fix after he heard all the stories. So he commanded all the beasts towards the spot. The man had heard them coming, so he came out from the hole of the tree and fled to save his life. All the animals broke the dead tree and searched out the hole. But nothing was to be found. But in the mind and heart of the tiger, he still feared the very words: 'Here comes the mighty Tapta.'

Eshei stepped out of her room. The hunger had given way to weariness and a dead ache that numbed her. The previous week she had woken up against the body of a strange man. The stranger had become her favourite bedfellow. The corner of her bed she shared with a stranger only pulled her towards itself. She was torn apart but only in her consciousness. Her subconscious had already moved on. She had given herself completely to a new sense of excitement that brought her sexual fulfillment and emotional empowerment. She ran to the light that was streaking into her life now. The bed was her new playground of emotions. The smell of his body was intoxicating. She could suddenly feel her arousal enveloping her thighs and hips. She raised herself to him and closed her eyes in anticipation of the pleasure she longed for. Nothing else mattered. She did not mind her lover's hurt and pain. She saw what she wanted to see.

The last time Eshei was home was when she came to confront the reality of her homeland. This time, it would be a confrontation with herself. Eshei had gone against her creed, her principles and this disbelief was what her immediate surrounding juxtaposed on her. Manipur's reality became her story.

It's a contradiction and a painful gangrene that was rotting the mind and the soul of a people who would say they have tried their best. Eshei was justified in her own way. She was patient and bearing, and she knew all the time that she would have to step aside but when the time came, she was vicious. Years of dysfunction does that to people.

The continents of disenchantment in personal lives and the public domain had arrested Manipur's daily life in a never-ending loop. Eshei was disenchanted by her love life and her career. She found her inability to help her family and friends very frustrating. But she forgot that in that frustration, she now needed to help herself. The entire system of the state was starkly similar to Eshei's predicament. They failed to comprehend that the symptoms of neglect that grows from their roots in the cracks in a wall, were finding a way into their lives.

A month passed without Eshei's presence in her promised homeland. Her father would expect the return of his favourite child and carry home the fish he imagined she always savoured. Her brother would sulk in the courtyard by the tulsi tree. Eshei would always tell him that she would spend time with him once she returned. Her mother knew that something was amiss this time. Her neighbours never really cared since she lost that fringe in her childhood. Personal loss is never measured in this place. Loss is inevitable. It is an expected consequence of life.

Eshei framed up her new black and white photograph and marked her entry into a new life: Da anouba photograph ama frame chanbado yamna wakhal leitaba malli – 'the new photograph framed up in the gallery of profiles is a picture of utter insensitivity.' Eshei's insensitivity was like a reflection of her surroundings. Her people would speak in a collective voice but often ignore the sensitivity of even a family member. Each person had become an island of anger and frustration. She did not have to meet any more expectations. She was ready to embark on her new job.

Her new accomplice had come with a mission. Eshei's

single goal now was to forget the past, do something for her homeland and pursue an invisible career. She had to rewrite the indigenous oral literature which she was so passionate about and slowly rework the assertion of this identity in her rendering of the folktales. She would receive no payment but her travel, food and lodging would be taken care of. She would attend seminars, organize workshops and meet people. Her job was about propaganda.

Most of the armed groups in her valley had become weary and the leadership was ageing. These outfits were no longer flush with income. Casualty was high and recruitment low. Propaganda was an obvious escape route to regroup under the banner of identity. Most groups across the region were following the same path.

It takes years to garner support for such a cause. Eshei was meant to take control of the frontal organizational work. They are called over-ground workers. They ensure they have no police cases and they elicit some amount of sympathy as well. They are preferably educated so that the outfit's ideology can be propagated. They love launching themselves under a human rights organization banner, picking up cases of army and police excesses and drumming up public outcry against the state.

Eshei took a different route. Her organization was meant to further folk art and literature and there could be no reason for suspicion. She took her life seriously but slowly. This work was not going to give instant results and change her generation's predicament. Her indoctrination now convinced her that she was preparing the next generation for a life free from Indian domination. Eshei's new job was to set right the historical subjugation of her people. Freedom songs are amongst the ancient anthems and Eshei was now buried in her search for that rhythm. Her freedom for her people would grant her the escape from her own past.

Everyone was looking for freedom from their own shackles. Armed groups were fighting for a separate homeland. Frontal organizations were fighting for a unified homeland. But land is premium here. Whose land is it anyway?

Eshei's freedom was an abstraction she could not have explained. It had all the trappings of her past. Her parents were still hoping their children would settle down like others. But for them settlement was not about a job and marriage.

Most children had left the state. Most of them looked back and longed for a slice of their childhood home. They also knew they had succumbed to this misplaced sense of freedom. Freedom from whom and what? In their search for their own space, many of them went their separate ways and some lost their way in the crowd.

Eshei started travelling to the capital again. It is here where she spent her formative years, but nothing of that era made any more sense in what she stood for today. The network of her people had taken root in the capital. She didn't have to work her way through that. It was an easy acceptance but Eshei's vision was beyond that. She had to theoretically justify the wrongs and earn the rights. Eshei's demeanour helped immensely. She paused before she spoke and her eyes had none of the emotion or angst that she planted in her mind. She was cold and manipulative in her looks; she could look as interested in naming a yellow mountain flower as much as in her lover's demise. But largely it was her disinterestedness that made her conspicuous.

Eshei was promoting an animation film based on a folktale from her childhood. The film was woven around four folktales but it was the tale of Sendrembi and Cheisra that consumed Eshei. There was a subconscious urge to identify with stories of deception. Eshei's photographic memory would not let her escape from the embroidered peacock which she wrapped around to bring herself luck. Her lover had got that woven for her but she deceived him even as she was accepting it from him. As usual, her eyes did not betray her intentions. This is a quality many of the liberation leaders would fall for.

The film opens in a mythological forest and a man is seen abandoning a child. His eyes are greedy and his hands are like a creature's. This is Ojaa. Kholiya's father, Ojaa breaks the promise he made to Kholiya's late mother – that he would take care of Kholiya and would not re-marry after her death. But he soon abandons her in the forest to be killed by wild animals and re-marries. However, Kholiya escapes and leads a happy life with an old couple. Ojaa and Kholiya are reconciled in the end. However, she refuses to accept him as her father and he is sent away with a gift, a magic cow. The cow accidentally kills his wife but Ojaa lives happily ever after.

The same forest reappears and Samoo Angoubagi Machanupi or the white elephant's daughter is seen sitting there. The beautiful but unfortunate girl and the prince of the land, fall in love with one another. The prince takes her to his kingdom to be married in pomp and ceremony. However, an ugly maid stops her at the palace gates and tricks her. The maid then impersonates her and becomes the queen and kills the white elephant's daughter.

But none of the deception of a lover was quite coming through in the tales and that was comforting for Eshei. Allegedly, her people were also tricked and betrayed into signing a treaty of accession. Betrayal is human history. Her own little private world of mistrust is just a speck in that narrative of deceit.

In the next sequence, Ngamtaban, a hunter, unwittingly marries a half-woman half-man tiger. The wife's kinsmen come to stay with them and find out that Ngamtaban has hunted and killed many of their kin. They plan to kill him but Ngamtaban ends up killing all of them – except his wife. She succeeds in killing him but meets her end when his faithful dog avenges his death.

Eshei's favourite tale of the two stepsisters took her back to the afternoons in the farmhouse of her childhood where discussions on liberation were not fashionable. That was when children would stay with their grandparents and listen to folktales and play war games like children do all over the world.

Once upon a time, there lived Sendrembi and Cheisra, two stepsisters with their widowed mothers. Sendrembi was the elder of the two and daughter of the first wife. After the death of their husband, the two widows worked hard to make both ends meet. Cheisra was the only child, while Sendrembi had a younger brother. Cheisra and her mother harboured intense hatred for Sendrembi and her mother. But Sendrembi and her mother never thought ill about Cheisra and her mother.

One day the two mothers took a laung (a kind of indigenous tool made of bamboo used to catch fish) each in their hands, tied tungons (an indigenous basket made of bamboo which is used for storing the captured fish) around their waists and went fishing at Silem Pat (a lake or a water body, which is bigger than a pond). Sendrembi's mother caught a tungon full of fish. Cheisra's mother caught only snakes and her tungon was filled with writhing baby snakes. At sunset they stopped fishing, came out of the water and rested beneath a heibong (Cluster fig in English, also called 'Goolar') tree. The ripe and juicy fruit that hung from the branches of the tree were quite tempting. Seeing them, Cheisra's mother exclaimed, 'Let's have some of these heibongs. I will pluck them.' She climbed the tree.

'I will drop ripe and yummy heibongs. Open your mouth sister,' she said cheerfully to Sendrembi.

Sendrembi's mother sat underneath the tree and opened her mouth. Cheisra's mother plucked a ripe heibong and dropped it into her mouth. Then she asked, 'Sister, was the ripe heibong good?' Sendrembi's mother managed to reply 'yes' with her mouth full.

Then she said, 'Okay! Then, I'll give you another one. This time open your mouth really wide.' Sendrembi's mother did as instructed, but instead of the fruit, the evil sister emptied her tungon inside out and poured all the snakes into her mouth.

Sendrembi's mother lay dead underneath the heibong tree, the snakebites had killed her. Cheisra's mother dumped her body in the lake, took away her tungon filled with fish, and went back home. When Sendrembi saw Cheisra's mother return alone, she asked anxiously, 'Where is mother? Why did she stay back?'

'Your wayward mother stayed behind in Silem Pat, saying she wants to catch some more fish,' retorted Cheisra's mother. Sendrembi and her brother were worried when their mother did not return that night. They started calling out her name and crying. Sendrembi did not have the courage to go searching for her mother at night. The laibak chaobi (laibak chaobi is 'the lucky girl.' This phrase, even though it is contradictory at this point, tells the audience that the girl Sendrembi will be lucky and is a blessed girl) Sendrembi could not eat anything and spent the whole night crying for her mother. Cheisra's mother scolded her for disturbing her sleep.

At dawn, the sad and tearful Sendrembi dozed off due to sheer exhaustion and the spirit of her dead mother came in her dreams and told her: 'My ebema Sendrembi, your stepmother poured snakes into my mouth and I have died from the snakebites. My five yaibi (the soul; in Manipur a person is supposed to have five souls, sometimes also called five lives) and life have turned into a tortoise in Silem Pat. Early tomorrow morning, come to the Pat with a laung in hand. Come and catch me without letting anyone know about it. Keep me in the esai–ephu (the pot used or storing water for everyday use) for five days. On the fifth day, I will try to recover my human form again and I will see if I can raise you and your brother.'

The moment Sendrembi woke up, she started calling for her mother and cried loudly. Cheisra's mother scolded her for waking her up and disturbing her sleep. Scared of her stepmother, Sendrembi cried quietly.

The next morning, Sendrembi entrusted her brother to her stepmother and went to Silem Pat with her laung. A tearful Sendrembi started fishing. She caught a ngamu (a kind of small and bony black fresh water fish. Its scientific name is Channa orientalis Schneider, and it is also called the 'walking snakehead.') Looking at it she said, 'Ha, ngamu radiant as fire! I did not come to catch you, I came to catch my Palem Ema.' (Both Ema and Palem means mother, here the phrase 'Palem Ema' means earthly mother). She released the ngamu into the water.

In this way, she caught and released many fish. At last, she caught the tortoise her mother turned into. Sendrembi wrapped the tortoise in a cloth and brought it home.

When Cheisra's mother asked her, 'How many fish did you catch?' She replied, 'Palem Ema, I did not catch any as I do not know how to fish,' and showed her the empty tungon. Afraid that Cheisra's mother might want to see the tortoise wrapped in her cloth, Sendrembi could hardly stand straight. When her stepmother told her to start cooking, she ran inside the house as fast as she could and put the tortoise in the esai-ephu.

Cheisra, who was hiding and observing Sendrembi, saw everything. She told her mother about it. The mother instructed her to demand and insist on drinking the water from the esai-ephu in the morning. The next morning Cheisra demanded to drink water in the esai-ephu. When Cheisra's mother told Sendrembi to give Cheisra some water, Cheisra cried out, 'Mai, Mai, I don't want to drink the water she has brought,' and pretended to cry.

The mother bit her lower lip and pretended to scold her. She said, 'Let her take the water on her own.' Cheisra, as planned by her mother, found the tortoise when she took the water and eventually handed the tortoise to her mother. The mother gave the tortoise to Sendrembi and said, 'Go and cook it, let's eat it.' Sendrembi did not say anything and started crying despondently. The stepmother scolded her for crying and accused Sendrembi of being mean. Terrified of her stepmother, the helpless Sendrembi wept silently and put the tortoise in a pot, lit the fire and started to boil her mother-turned-tortoise.

On being heated, the tortoise in the pot cried out, 'Emagi, ebema Sendrembi, my feet are burning.' Sendrembi pulled out the firewood and cried. Seeing this Cheisra complained, 'Ema, ema, sister Sendrembi has pulled out the firewood and is crying instead of boiling the tortoise.' 'Slap her face,' replied Cheisra's mother. Afraid of her stepmother, Sendrembi lit the fire again. Unable to bear the heat, the tortoise cried out, 'Ebema,my daughter, the fire has reached my waist, my chest, my neck and I'm finished.' With that, the tortoise breathed her last inside the pot. Sendrembi stretched out her body and feet, and cried. She also refused to eat the tortoise. Cheisra and her mother ate the whole tortoise and threw the bones in the backyard.

That night, her mother came again in Sendrembi's dream and told her, 'Ebema! Collect all my bones and keep it in your phiruk (a basket made of bamboo that is broad and low. Today, a phiruk is usually used for religious purposes) covered with a cloth for seven days.' Sendrembi did as she was instructed without letting Cheisra and her mother know about it. On the sixth day, Sendrembi became curious to know whether her mother had come to life or not, lifted the cloth to check. Since a mortal had laid eyes on the remains before the stipulated seven days were over, her mother could not become human; she became a swallow and flew away. Seeing this, Sendrembi cried out at the top of her voice calling for her mother.

Years passed, both Sendrembi and Cheisra grew up. One day, Sendrembi dressed in torn phanek and old phi (a scarf that is wrapped around the upper body) and Cheisra dressed in new phanek and phi went to fetch water with a puun (pot used for fetching water with a narrow mouth and long neck) each. While they were walking, they met King Tukaoba who had come hunting. Even though she was wearing a torn phanek and an old phi, Sendrembi's beauty impressed the king. The king came near her and requested her to give him some water to drink. Afraid of her stepmother, Sendrembi requested the king to drink the water brought by her sister Cheisra. On hearing her words, the disappointed and embarrassed king left without drinking water. Cheisra narrated everything to her mother when they returned. The next day, the stepmother made Cheisra wear Sendrembi's torn phanek and old phi, and Sendrembi, Cheisra's new clothes.

When the two sisters returned after fetching water, they met King Tukaoba at the same place, waiting for Sendrembi. The king could not take away his eyes off Sendrembi, now dressed in beautiful clothes. The king rode up to Sendrembi and asked her to give him some water to drink. Cheisra seethed with anger. Afraid of her stepmother, Sendrembi refused. With tears in her eyes, Sendrembi requested him to drink water from her sister. The king replied, 'I want to drink the water you have brought. Please give me a little water and satisfy my thirst.' The king repeatedly requested her to give him some water. Finally, unable to bear his entreaties anymore, Sendrembi took down her water pot, said, 'Here, here, drink your fill,' and passed the pot to the king. Instead of taking the pot Sendrembi offered him, King Tukaoba grabbed her hand, pulled her up on his horse and rode away. Cheisra dropped the pot on the ground and ran to her house. She narrated the whole incident to her mother.

Sendrembi became the queen, Cheisra and her mother led a miserable life. The innocent and virtuous Sendrembi led a happy life. The next year she gave birth to a son. Cheisra and her mother invited Sendrembi for a feast.

Sendrembi took permission from the king and came for the feast. The son stayed with his father. At sunset, after food and rest, Sendrembi decided to return to the palace and began searching for her clothes. She found Cheisra wearing them. She remarked, 'Ebema I will go now, my son must be crying for me. Give me my clothes sister.' Cheisra took off the clothes and threw them under the bed and refused to retrieve them. The moment Sendrembi bent down to retrieve her clothes, Cheisra poured boiling hot water that her mother had secretly heated. Sendrembi breathed her last instantly.

Her five lives turned into chekla lamkhunu – a wild wood pigeon and flew away. Perched on the sandangkha, (a traditional A-shaped Manipuri hut, the protruding part of the thatch keeps away the rain and sun in the front as well as the back of the hut) Sendrembi saw her lifeless body and cried helplessly. The wood pigeon flew away sorrowfully when she saw Cheisra's mother looking for a stick to kill her. Cheisra wore Sendrembi's clothes and jewels and went to the king impersonating Sendrembi. When she reached, Cheisra did not go near the king. When he saw her ugly face, he got suspicious and inquired, 'Ebema, what happened? Today after your mother's feast you have come back with your eyes sunken and heels all cracked.'

Cheisra replied like Sendrembi would have, 'Sabi ningthou ebungo, (sabi means a young man, ningthou means the king and ebungo is the masculine equivalent of ebema) I worried that my little son must be crying for me so I came running and my heels cracked. Remembering my dead parents, I cried calling out their names and my eyelashes became uneven and jagged. And pressing and wiping out my tears has sunken my eyes.' In his heart of hearts, the king was still suspicious. In this way many days passed with the king still suspicious about his wife. One day the King's sajik-loi – servant who cuts fodder-grass for the royal horse – was busy in his work when Sendrembi-turned-wood pigeon came and sat upon the branches of a big tree nearby and started singing:

Krooku ku-ku khangmeitat
Ha! King's sajik-loi
Go and entreat your Goddess!
Go and entreat your Lord!
With all the essential fruits!
And all obligatory prints in the clothes!
Don't let any harm come to my son, the king
If you do not report what I say
I will destroy your sickle,
I will cause you harm,
And bring you ruin.
Sendrembi sitting on top of the tree,
Cheisra occupying the royal throne.
Ha, Ningthou Tukaoba!
Have you forgotten your queen-wife?
Kookru ku-ku khangmeitat!

On hearing the wood pigeon speak in a human language, the sajik-loi dropped his sickle and ran as fast as he could to the king. He reported everything to the king. At that very moment the wood pigeon flew over and perched herself on the sandangkha. On seeing the wood pigeon, the king looked at it affectionately and said, 'Ha, chekla, if you have been created out of the five lives of Sendrembi then come and have these grains of rice in my hands.' The bird flew down from the sandangkha and started eating the rice. The king then caught the wood pigeon and kept it in a cage. Sendrembi came in the king's dream, 'Sabi Eningthou (Eningthou means my king or in other words 'my lord.' Note the difference between the way Sendrembi and Cheisra address the king. Sendrembi calls the king 'my king' while Cheisra calls him 'king' like everybody else does) ebungo, keep the wood pigeon born from my five lives away from mortal eyes and knowledge. On the seventh day, I will try to become human again and see whether I can raise our son.' And so the king kept the wood pigeon carefully away from mortal eyes.

One day, when the king went hunting with his entourage, Cheisra killed the wood pigeon and made chagempomba (a Manipuri dish cooked with an assortment of green vegetables, broken rice, fermented soybean and fish or meat. Chagem means the broken rice and pomba is a way of cooking) out of it. Seeing the empty cage on his return, the king questioned Cheisra about the bird. Cheisra replied that she got angry at the wood pigeon for scaring her son, so she killed it and made chagempomba out of it. The king got very angry. He scolded Cheisra and she had to throw away the chagempomba.

After some time, at the place the chagempomba was thrown away, the flesh and bones of the pigeon grew into a mango tree. The tree grew bigger and bigger and bore only one beautiful mango. The king protected the mango carefully and did not let anyone pluck it. One day the king's sajik-loi came searching for a fruit and saw the mango. He took the permission of the queen, plucked the fruit and took it home to eat it. The moment he reached his house, the king sent his messengers and called for him. So he put the mango in his chenphu (a big pot, essential to every Manipuri household regardless of tribe or community, kept in the kitchen for storing rice. Cheng is rice and phu is short for chaphu which is pot) and went to the king.

The next day he remembered the mango and decided to eat it. But he could not find a knife and left it for the next day. The following day, he found the knife but forgot where he kept the mango. In this way, if he had the knife, he did not have the fruit, and if he had the fruit, there was no knife; days passed. On the night of the seventh day, the mango turned into a beautiful young girl. The next day, the moment the sajik-loi went to cut grass, the girl came out and cooked for him. After arranging the house properly and completing all the chores, she would go to a corner and hide. The sajik-loi was very surprised at this. He asked his neighbors but none of them had cooked food for him. He became suspicious. He wondered which god was trying to punish him. So he decided to find out and capture whoever had been cooking for him – whether it was a mortal, a spirit, or a god. He went out of the house with sickle in his hands, came back secretly, and hid himself.

Thinking that she was alone, the young girl came out of her hiding place and started cooking. When she was cooking, the man ran towards her and almost grabbed her wrist when the girl stood up and said 'I am Sendrembi.' She narrated all the incidents of the past and the way in which she had become a human again. The man believed her and ran to the king to inform him. The king sent his messengers and brought Sendrembi to the court. In front of all his subjects, the king gave Sendrembi and Cheisra a holy sword each and put them to a test. First, Cheisra struck Sendrembi with the holy sword but nothing happened. Sendrembi took the sword and struck Cheisra. The evil Cheisra died instantly. With Cheisra's death, Sendrembi became the queen of the land again. The king and the queen lived happily ever after.

Eshei had a job at hand and as she arranged the first screening of the film, she realized that her mission was tediously long. In the large auditorium, the audience was tiny and the empty seats indicated the amount of work she had ahead of her.

Film distributors turned down requests of running the film in theatres. They said animation didn't work in India. Besides, the characters are alien to Indian mainland culture so while *Hanuman* ran full house, this film would not be economically viable. So how did *The Lion King* run? Oh, that was in English. So if they dubbed this film in English would it run?

Eshei found even more reason to dissect it under the tint of her ethnicity. Mainland India wasn't yet ready to accept her culture. She looked different (not that a turbaned Sikh bears any similarity with anybody else in this country), her cuisine was different and now she discovered that even her folktales were different. So what was she doing here? This was exactly the point her leaders were making.

Eshei never enjoyed tea even though one of her closest friends owned a tea estate. She was herself confused with the question of identity and culture when she looked back at how much interest she took in her roommate's cultural identity. She knew nothing about the Assamese way of life even though she had lived four years of her life with her. So why was she peeved that film distributors were saying that her culture was not known to the larger audience?

As long as the periphery remains the periphery, the mutinies will continue. But when one is on the periphery then the centre is as far as Eshei is from the centre. It balances out, and within the periphery one finds similar stories of alienation.

Power cuts are so common in her hometown that the day-long load shedding in the capital is something that hardly bothered Eshei. Her campaigns are now more urban than the villages she talks about, her protest marches are on clean pavements rather than on the dirt tracks of her homeland. She had liberated herself from all the bondages of human emotion and her sense of reason would not betray her again.

Eshei developed new interests or maybe she revived old ones. She was suddenly the town's new exhibitionist. She posed for photographs like a cheap, pavement poster girl. She, the otherwise fiercely private person, was now flaunting her new status. She could now hold her lover's hand and step out but every step that she took was yet another stamp of confusion. She could never agree to killing anyone for money or ideology. She gave up meat because she couldn't bear animal sacrifice. And here she was aligned with the most brutal minds on earth. People who have killed thousands and haven't winced once. People who kill and justify it as sacrifice for a cause. She tightened her grip on his arm and pulled him closer.

Her rucksack contained a moisturizer, lip-gloss, soap, and comb. Her cosmetics end here. A few satin undergarments tucked on both sides, her shorts and tops. The green phanek, ankle length jeans, socks, slippers. The maroon dress and whatever was already in the bag. She didn't forget her favourite book, *The Little Prince*. Eshei was on the move again.

FIFTEEN

The Lost Tribe

In a region where you can lose count of the number of tribes and sub-tribes, there is also a lost tribe. More than 7000 Bnei Menashes in India's north-east claim they are the one of the 'lost tribes of Israel.'

A Thanksgiving ceremony is taking place at the Khongsai household. They belong to the Bnei Menashe, the Jewish tribe found in Manipur and Mizoram. After seeking affiliation from Israel since the seventies, the Bnei Menashes have finally been recognized by the Chief Rabbi of the Shepardic Jews in Israel. Many Bnei Menashes have already migrated to Israel with the help of a US-based organization. Many of them are settled in the Gaza Strip.

Nili Hangshing proudly displayed massive photo albums of his daughter's wedding in Jerusalem, from where he had just returned. The pride was about a conceived homeland where he could get his daughter married. The idea of 'homeland' is the strongest emotion in these parts and even if that seems mythical, the assertion is unavoidable.

The return of the 'lost tribes' to their ancient homeland is viewed by some as the fulfillment of a biblical prophecy and a heralding of the Messiah, made centuries ago. They sing in Hebrew and follow all customs and traditions of the Jews. But to stumble on an entire locality of Jews in the middle of Churachandpur is bit of a cultural and religious detour.

According to the Old Testament, during the reign of King Solomon, the tribes of Israel split into two kingdoms, Israel in the north and Judea in south. In 723 BC the Assyrians conquered the kingdom of Israel and sent ten of the twelve biblical tribes into exile; they dispersed all over the world. The Bnei Menashes of the north-east are said to be one of these lost tribes of Israel.

All that we could find out from elders like Hoshia was very little in terms of information: 'As told by my father and grandfather, most of our tribals in the eastern regions in India come from China and Tibet. Then I found our story – how we belong to the tribe of Menashe. It's because of our traditions, sacrifical rituals, they claim that our forefathers had descended from one of the tribes of Israel. There is no documented evidence but we know that we belong to Menashe.'

Despite being here for centuries, the Bnei Menashes' customs, including mourning rites, hygiene and the use of a lunar calendar, closely mirror Jewish traditions.

Going to Israel is a moment the Bnei Menashes wait for.

We saw that there were more than 100 students learning Hebrew at the Churachandpur Centre and there are five more centres around Manipur that teach Hebrew and the Jewish way of life.

The acceptance by the Chief Rabbi of the Shepardic Jews in Israel that the Bnei Menashes of Manipur and Mizoram are in fact, one of the ten lost tribes of Israel, is an acceptance of their Jewish identity – but the sanction by the Rabbi doesn't necessarily mean the Israeli government will recognize the conversions and allow immigration. That is of little importance to the Bnei Menashes; they have only been waiting for this spiritual acceptance.

SIXTEEN

Angami in a Saree

'Yes, get me tea, green, with milk and mint. So that it looks like we're having milk and cookies. Seeing the lack of colour in our cups, the casual observer will assume our conversation to be trivial, even juvenile chit-chat and render us invisible. Then unheard and unseen, we will carry on, secretly conjuring up shades of purple and nibble on them.'

Keze had her face turned to the window which looked eastwards into the unknown mountain. Her shaven head made her look like a monk who had realized the futility of struggle. In the ancient land, unmarried Angami girls would shave their heads. Looking at her, it's not difficult to gauge why. She drew everyone's attention.

'How much sugar? Ummm … sips of angry maroon Assam punctuated with nibbles of dark-purple pitha and the rains … now I really miss home.'

Pitha comes in various shapes and sizes, and colours as

well. The purple one is particularly delicious. It's almost shapeless. Its sweetness is just about right and when bitten into, a dull rice flavour fills the mouth. It's a little oily on the surface but Keze loves them. She makes sure her arrangement in the hills has a regular supply of them.

She loved the off-white saree, the one with the red border. An unusual choice in Nagaland. The blouse would hang reluctantly on her body. But her charm lay in the unassuming manner in which she carried it off. She wanted to be draped in the saree and be served dinner, followed by tea. After the engaging evening, Blue Hills as she liked calling herself, never returned – as if she left these pages as suddenly as she had appeared. When I last heard of her, she was still writing her favourite food column about 'smoked khungsha cooked in anishe with raja and khuvie tathu and ga kemeluo.'

Some people are never seen and known beyond a few paragraphs. Keze walked in like a cloud from the hills and left unnoticed. Nagaland has been an elusive journey. So much of it is known and seen and read and yet, that veil of unfamiliarity clouds the hills.

SEVENTEEN

The Tea Party

In the late 1970s, Assam was perpetually in darkness. The Assam agitation meant blackouts, curfew and clashes.

One evening, the student leaders had announced 'Nishpradip' which means no light. Young Assam was suddenly rebellious and the light of another freedom movement spurred them on. Leaders of this movement were born overnight in every dark alley. How many Indian streets in the 70s had lights, anyway?

A few volunteers intercepted a motorbike which had its headlights on. By their diktat, it was a 'no light' evening and everyone listened to them. Incidentally, the motorcycle was a police vehicle so those boys were promptly arrested without much fuss.

The next day, two friends of the arrested volunteer were returning home after paying a visit at the police station. Police stations were converted into makeshift hostels with more and more volunteers pouring in.

As the two friends of the 'political prisoners' were heading back home after their patriotic visit, they heard a car screech behind them. Instinctively, they ran. It was a police jeep.

The cops gave a chase. One of the boys entered a lane adjacent to the Guwahati College and found himself at a dead end. There were hutments around so he lay on the ground along the corridor, inside a cluster of rooms meant for labourers. In those days, labourers in Assam meant people from Bihar. He pressed himself against the bamboo wall of the labour quarters. A pair of shoes brushed against his feet. The policemen searched with torch lights and checked all the rooms and left. One of the inmates came out with a lantern and finding a man lying on the floor, screamed. He was gagged and pushed aside. This was routine. Police and students would encounter each other with increasing ferocity.

The Assam agitation led by students' organizations had reached a frenetic pace. But the seriousness of it all was watered down by the mode in which the agitation played out. The agitation was codenamed 'Swabalambi' or self-sufficiency, but that assumed a different meaning altogether.

No apparent ideology guided the movement. The people who supported the Congress were ostracized and even abused. Those who leaned to the Left were considered traitors. Three decades after Independence, the country was witnessing a mass regional movement. It was momentous, but without a guiding spirit, it was floundering.

The competition to perform was almost perverse. Each locality had clubs and all clubs were potential party headquarters of the students' union. The slogans and the frustration were shared, but the leadership emerged from a bunch of uninspired minds that shaped the destiny of Assam for the next thirty years. The agitation was more of intimidation.

One day, members of Club 11 hijacked a bus from the main road. Drove it to a petrol station and filled up the fuel tank and obviously made no pretense of making the payment. Then they drove to Fancy Bazaar, the city's commercial hub. There was nothing fancy about the market, it was just a wicked twist to the original name, 'Phashi Bazaar,' which meant the market for hanging. The central jail was located here. Here, they collected 'donations', money coerced from the civilians. Half of that donation was distributed as flood relief to some nearby village and the rest was their allowance. This practice soon became an institutionalized form of employment across the region.

The frontline members of this movement were not moved by any high ideals and many of them were half-educated. On one occasion, in a heated oratorical exercise, a leader of the Asom Gana Sangram Parishad countered accusations of being 'bourgeoisie' and he went on to say : 'Though they call us bourgeoisie we haven't yet "drowned" and are still afloat.' It didn't make any sense to his audience. Most of what the student leaders said was not loaded with meaning. But the crowd was bemused and believed they were making sense. The leader had no idea what the word meant in English because bourgeoisie in Assamese means 'to sink' and he was only clarifying that the agitation is still in flow!

Nicknamed Handyman, one volunteer was told by his friends that a new sensation, Hakimoni, had arrived in the locality and was only available to studs. Handyman approached the shanty where Hakimoni lived. The friends had made arrangements to watch the performance when Handyman had only lifted one end of the blanket and out came a thick mustached male face, petrified by an agitator's attempted molestation. Embarrassed, Handyman took out his anger on this poor man who was only a construction labourer. Workforce in Assam then was predominantly from Bihar and they were the soft targets for the vanguards of Assamese sub-nationalism.

Some days later, Handyman led a procession with slogans against the Indian state, accusing the government of dominating and oppressing the people of Assam, who would not tolerate the subjugation any longer.

In neighbouring Meghalaya, another chauvinist students' movement was fomenting. A strategist of that union, Crowbore had come from the Shillong Students' Union to forge an alliance with the Assam Students' Union and had brought with him a roadmap for a collaborative rebellion, for which they would seek foreign help. The seeds for the regional alliance were being sown. Crowbore was taken to the Cotton College where he met two leaders of the agitation who are now a lawyer and a minister. The meeting could not even begin. Crowbore could speak only in English and Khasi and the leaders did not dare utter any English, so the secret closed-door meeting was called off due to the lack of a common language or an interpreter.

The alliance, however, would be entered into at a later date. The common target was the invisible illegal Bangladeshi migrant who was apparently everywhere, but couldn't be identified. So everyone who did not belong to the dominant community felt the heat of a xenophobic mass movement which had lost its direction even before it reached anywhere. Hidden in its confusion were the first seeds of an armed rebellion.

Babulal's parantha shop was the official round table for policy decisions of the students. So he had to cater to young intellectuals deciding the course of Assam's future. One day, Babulal declared that he could not carry on without payment for his services. The students who were all self-styled leaders found Babul's refusal to be an act of audacity. Babulal was the symbol of the oppressor who was getting richer with the hard-earned money of the indigenous people. Punishment was inevitable.

Babulal's posterior was subjected to a itchy wild bush, locally known as 'bandarkekura.' It's like poison ivy. Babulal filed an FIR of attempt to murder. The shop finally closed down. Like many of his kin, Babulal too left for home.

Though the Congress and Left parties were taboo, the agitation had a right wing and left wing along with a militant wing as well. Self-styled (this term later became the most abused word in official documents and continues to be so) explosive experts arrived one day at Noonmati in Guwahati to impart lessons on explosive making. After the agitation ended, one of the explosive experts became a successful cinematographer who drank himself to death.

One variety of the explosives was made of petrol and soap. But none of those bombs ever worked. Cast iron pipes were stolen from the nearby oil refinery to manufacture pipe guns but even those didn't fire. This was the beginning of Assam's militancy.

Schools and colleges had shut down and the state was thrown into a state of anarchy. The administration had no control whatsoever and their actions only aggravated the situation. But anecdotes from those street fighting years are often hilarious.

'Tez dim tel ni diu' or 'We will give blood but not oil' was the punch line of the agitation. Groups of hundreds of thousands of agitators of all ages would take to the streets and shout, 'Aeijui jolise, jolisei, joliboi' (the fire is raging, raging and will keep raging). The leaders played to the gallery with silly similies and their favourite butt of jokes was the then-President of India. On one occasion, a leader was applauded for saying that the 'President hides himself under the Prime Minister's mekhela.'The baton of the CRPF was compared with match sticks in another popular slogan: 'CRPF-er lathi deshlai kathi.'

One day, when an entire locality left for the day's dharna, a few young couples slipped out for a rendezvous. Dharnas were like picnics with soaked gram which is a snack as well as an offering in religious occasions in these parts. Bengali newspapers had even taken a dig at it, calling it a 'gram agitation.' The reaction was predictable. Bengali localities were attacked with stones and a few houses were set on fire. Arson is a very popular weapon that accompanies frustration. These couples wanted a day out, so they chose a local school to frolic in. Schools and colleges were all shut down. After all, this was a students' movement.

Proud guardians had no problem with their children staying out of schools and institutions. The time had arrived for the freedom movement.

Just as the happy hour had started for our passion-filled friends, a group of agitators walked into the school to hold a routine meeting and found these young couples in a rather intimate position. The meeting was cancelled. These young men and women were branded anti-nationals and were even beaten. How could they think of sex when the identity of the Asomiya was at stake? The agitation, however, was one of the most emancipating sexual events in the modern history of Assam. Boys and girls were suddenly in the midst of a liberating exchange not of ideas as much as companionship. With educational institutions shut down and families joining in the agitation, the youngsters too had the permission to step out. The rites of courtship had now become more physical. Young Assam was going through a sexual revolution of sorts.

The agitation went out of control in Dispur, the capital. Every day, the battle was getting intense. Thousands of agitators would wait for police action; to counter it with non-violent means which often turned violent. The police would fire tear gas to disperse mobs and the students would hit back. They would catch the teargas shells with a wet cloth and throw them back. The violence escalated.

But the recipe of agitation was wrong. Neither was it credibly led. By evening the boys would gather for potluck. The tear gas shells gave away to merrymaking. Goats would be stolen from the neighbourhood and cooked in watery gravy and the freedom fighters would sit around the enormous pot of mutton, joking about the eventful day.

One evening, Noonmati club boys arrived in a nearby locality, Gandhibasti. The hosts had to outdo the hospitality that the guests had accorded to them earlier. The evening was a wild boys' night out.

Sarma had remained largely disinterested in this agitation, ignoring snide remarks from his peer group. Till he met a martial arts guru who was an active votary of the movement. Sarma's involvement suddenly grew several folds and overnight, he became a leader. One training that volunteers received was to be alert to the sound of police jeeps. One fateful morning when the dingy boats had arrived with varieties of fish at the Narengi Ghat, a convoy of police jeeps made their way to Sarma's home. The sound travelling from a winding hill road had woken him up and he escaped to the backyard garden. The police had the bunglow surrounded from all sides, as if they had come to arrest the kingpin of the movement. Sarma's father calmly handed his son over to the police. A group of

Malayali CRPF constables took him away, engaging him in a conversation regarding the futility of the movement. At the police station, a few others were waiting and the police officer, in an inimitable accent and posture, explained how Mahanta and Phukan (the leaders of the people) will be feasting on chicken legs, while the bones will be thrown to people like Sarma. It turned out to be quite a prophetic statement.

Sarma was then moved to the district court lockup – a jungle of criminals and patriots struggling to occupy space. Sarma knew he had to do something dramatic to survive in that climate. It was his first jail tour. So he hurled a few abuses and perched himself up on a half-wall which separated the hardcore criminals from the lesser known ones. And then he urinated on the crowd of criminals. This shock therapy worked. He was immediately accepted in the fold. Sarma was bailed out the following day. He returned to his locality as a leader who suffered a jail term and in the next one year, he was engaged in Swabalambi activities like making paper bags and selling fish. Sarma was still not a member of the students' union but was actively involved in picketing and road blockades and beating up people who did not support the agitation such as members of the Left party.

Three decades later, Sarma regrets some of his acts and has gone around looking for the people he had abused back then and to apologize. That is a rare gesture.

Organizations like Purbanchaliya Lok Parishad, Assam Jatiyabadi Yuva Chatra Parishad, All Assam Students' Union took the lead in freeing Assam from the shackles of 'Indian colonial occupation.' In this sub-national aggression was hidden the seed of anti-nationalism that fuelled ULFA. They would argue it was 'nationalism.'

When ULFA was baptized somewhere in Upper Assam, it came across as another youth organization which meant business. The story they later circulated of their oath taking on the ramparts of the Rang Ghar, the Ahom royal palace was an intelligent way of ensuring support. It was symbolic. But beyond the symbol and its hatred against the establishment, it was a dangerous organism being fuelled by popular opinions.ULFA was formed by default. Not a design. Their terrorist avatar was also a coincidence. The agitation against suspected foreigners from Bangladesh lapsed into communal clash within Indian communities. The communal divide was transformed into ethnic aspirations. Aspirations which spiralled into an era of instability.

Then began the unending serial killing episodes of ULFA. Assam slipped into an unbelievable abyss of regression and violence. I arrived here amidst a mad cycle of murders. My first recollection is of a deserted street in Nalbari.

It was Diwali. The temple bells were ringing at an odd hour when the killers sprayed bullets on people celebrating the festival of lights. A little girl ran out of a half-down shop shutter. She had sustained a bullet injury below her left knee. For years, I could see this little girl with a fresh wound running through my mind.

Indiscriminate killing continued without any resistance. Low intensity violence is invariably reduced to statistics and that was the guerilla warfare technique that ULFA mastered.

For more than thirty years the organization maintained its chain of command and kept manipulating, raising illegal money, striking at will and terrorizing common people. But the ULFA leadership or the think tank could not have been so sharp in their strategy to sustain such a protracted insurgency. What may have been their strength is probably hidden in the weaknesses of the system in which the country functions.

The indirect beneficiaries of conflict are so widespread that combating insurgency became the most lucrative cycle of black economy.

The commander of ULFA, a former Indian Railways porter got the job on a sports quota. He was a footballer. He was on the payroll of the Railways for a long time, even though his attendance sheet would be marked absent for thirty years. His salary pay slips were issued till someone noticed it.

Terrorism or revolution, this leader knew little about either. But when he was introduced to this idea, he took over and held on to the top position for decades. He ran a multi-crore fishing and trawler business in Bangladesh and struck international arms deals on high seas. He is supposed to have changed his religion and circumcized his sons in order to enlist support of the Islamic militant groups or as Indian agencies claim, the Inter-Services Intelligence in Pakistan. He has evaded arrest, detention and even managed not to reveal his face to the rest of the world. Indian agencies have just a few of his old photographs which are flashed for any reference to his activities. In one, he is looking happy with a moustache revealing nothing of his guerilla nature. In another, he is walking along with some colleagues in a camp in Bhutan without his uniform. And a third, where he is sitting cross-legged on a bed with a colleague and playing chess. It's only in 2011 when he finally released a video of himself dancing during Bihu with his cadres, where he exposed his face. Ageing, but he still held on to his beliefs.

The rest is all presumptuous. Leaders such as Mr Footballer have become recipes of urban legends. We were fed with stories of his fitness regime; he could walk forty-five kilometres and he played football at the Dhaka cantonment every morning at four. Or the foreign secretary trained in public diplomacy from Philipines, who went as far as the UN to address his case but was later found to actually teach yoga in a Dhaka locality to make ends meet. Information on all these are never substantiated and generally fed to the media who accept it without cross-checking their authenticity.

Insurgency is complex and at the same time, boring to elaborate. It has provided food for so many people in this region that the biggest employment generation element in this state and the surrounding ones comes from insurgency. I prefer calling it terrorism. Some say 'underground.' Others say 'separatist movements.' In the absence of clarity, semantics have played a very significant role in the history of insurrections.

The police get additional funds to fight insurgency. Paramilitary and army are paid by the state to aid the state police forces. The popular belief is that their unaudited source-money helps them accrue retirement benefits. Allied companies, for example, the food chains supplying to the large presence of security forces monopolize their business with hefty kickbacks. Human rights organizations are funded by international and national fundraisers. Centres of peace and conflict have sprouted and mushroomed around us. All forms of subversive business from gunrunning, wildlife smuggling to narcotics to car theft thrive under such regimes. The armed groups themselves create more and more sub-groups to abduct against ransom, extort and invest in businesses. They surrender and get into major government contracts, where they obviously make money. Many of them run for elections which legitimizes every terror act they might have committed. It gives them power and public funds for their private pleasures. Mediators of these peace parleys are also beneficiaries of money that is floating for development and peace. Why leave the media which feeds incessantly on this chronic ailment and publicizes it to no end?

Eshei would have preferred to stay away but her circumstances drove her to search for a cause to live. Hundreds of Esheis also found a reason to live.

These fragments I have shored against my ruins
Why then Ile fit you. Hieronymo's mad againe.
Datta. Dayadhvam. Damyata.
Shantih shantih shantih

TS Eliot

EIGHTEEN

Markets

'You see Guwahati is a "relentlessly" ugly city,' as a Foreign Service officer from Delhi's Defence Colony married to a local boy had once put it. But to be fair to its founders, it's also pretty in patches.

The city has a daily vegetable market on the banks of the Brahmaputra. It's often a Sunday morning past-time for the city's senior crowd. I have considered an opinion about it from time to time, but after the debacle of choosing another market (a suggestion that I sought for no reason), I have decided to stick to my opinion for a hundredth time, that Cachari market on a Sunday morning is a good idea. Both the markets have their own loyal clientele.

The market I chose or rather, was suggested to me, was the Colony Market which has a few other nicknames: Bamunimaidan market or Kolong Paar market, named after the train that passes by this market carrying local produce. It's an area in the east of Guwahati, a typically crowded colony of railway employees, where the urban laws are a little different.

They are a world unto their own. Red brick British era double-storey houses with high ceilings. Illegal constructions are almost acceptable. Sub-letting out government accommodations to outsiders is quite common.

Most railway colonies are dominated by a certain type of Bengali-speaking people who dress and speak in a similar manner. They are found in almost all railway colonies across the country. That's because when the railway was introduced, the babus that the Bristish employed were from Bengal. Bamunimaidan, however, has a decent distribution of Assamese people too who have acquired the quintessential railway colony persona. An insider once shared her thoughts: 'Railway colonies had a hierarchical structure a little dissimilar from cantonment. As in they were often in the midst of town or towns that came up around their supply of goods.Which means for a railway kid a passing train was both a routine beauty and a sound that stays in the memory, long after the railway childhood is over. Also while these were colonies, they allowed the discovery of talent, a club life, some Indianized "sahibji" things like dances, bridge and the precious bonhomie unlike other civil services. A sub-culture all by itself.'

This colony also has a history of harbouring and producing some of the city's militant cadres, who have since surrendered or moved out. From being quite a hub of militant activities and anti-social engagement, the colony has retained much of its character. For a few years, the militants used this as a favourite place for carrying out low-intensity blasts not because they disliked the people but because they found it easier to mingle in the crowd and escape. The roads are narrow and crammed with shops ranging from old books to ingredients of any puja that Bengalis and Assamese have in the Panjika, their pink book of auspicious dates and events. In fact, this dark pink manual with a lot of graphic designs on its cover jacket is an annual publication and a very important decision-maker on travel dates and guides people with their planetary configuration. If I had consulted this essential 'lonely planet' guide, perhaps my Sunday morning disappointment could have been averted.

The geography of the market is a maze because most of it is run illegally. It has two main entrances. Three more subways can lead you to the mandi. From the main entrance, shops carrying chicken in massive round cane baskets are in display. That merges into a row of essential commodity shops. The smell of broiler chicken and incense is a heady mix. The bird sellers are Bengali Muslims while the other shops are run by Bengali Hindus. The Muslims are definitely not indigenous railway colony insiders.

A concrete construction leads you to the first fish and meat market. I have found them dubious for no good reason and so I generally avoid this row of shops. An adjacent vegetable market sells the usual. The vegetable market has an extension of items like brooms, earthenware and several other things which have become extinct in other parts of the world.

Beyond this lies another three layers of vegetables and one of fish. The most interesting market is the one on the railway tracks. The Kolong Paar Express brings fresh vegetables and fish from Kolong in Central Assam and slows down around this area for an organized racket to supply vegetables to petty vendors. It's fresh and cheap.

But to sit before each variety and pluck out a brinjal or a green papaya from a crowd and with ugly hands pawing at the vegetables, is an utterly disgusting experience. So the day I went horribly wrong and chose to visit this market, I quickly and sheepishly picked up a few moolis, karela, one brinjal and a bagful of cauliflowers. I convinced myself that it was a dream bargain and so the grime and chaos was worth it.

The second fish market closer to the railway track has smaller varieties of lachin bhangon, shorputhi etc. The first one makes an Assamese delicacy called masor tenga or sour fish, which an Assamese would consider a Sunday afternoon delight. Actually an all-time delight. For the Bengali, this fish preparation would amount to wasting the holiday. So tenga is one of several aspects that separate these two communities who share a love-hate relationship. The love quotient has increased several times over the last two decades. But tenga can sour it instantly!

The Cachari market is more of an outing. Situated on the river banks in a corner plot of land, it's open and happy. The pedestrian sidewalk from where the market finds its point of entry has a spread of local dahi in earthen pots, covered with banana leaves and tied with natural fibres.

A family sits near a cluster of fresh green coconuts with plastic straws. Homegrown herbs and homemade snacks are laid out neatly along the pavement. One or two ducks also make their way to this row of shops. On a concrete pedestal right at the entrance sits a lady who appears to have aged in her prime. She has an assortment of spinach and herbs like dhania and pudina along with small local chicken eggs which sell at a higher price than the ones from the farm or in other words, commercial poultry.

Cane baskets and rice-cleaning platters in various sizes are also on sale. The vendors who occupy the footpath bring a little produce from their tiny garden which doesn't qualify as cultivation but earns them a little something. They come from the other bank of the Brahmaputra with banana flowers and stems, a bunch of some vegetables, small round dark green pumpkins and even pumpkin flowers.

Mr Saikia the retired bureaucrat and Mr Bezbaruah, the city's most respected journalist are already surveying the products with a very keen eye, touching them to gauge the freshness and taste. A ripe papaya, for example, must have some of the sticky discharge on the stem to indicate that it's fresh from the tree and not ripened at home.

Inside the market in neat rows are vegetable and fruit vendors. On one side, potato and onions can be purchased at wholesale rates, slightly cheaper than the retail price. Each shop is on a raised plot of earth covered well with bio-degradable material. So it's a very eco-friendly market. Mohamed Salim takes an early morning bus from Singimari with at least fifteen different varieties of saag or leafy products and if asked, he can explain how each one is cooked. For example, babari is cooked with duck eggs.

Mr Das, the city's oldest resident who still makes it for an afternoon game of tennis, won't forget to pick up his own bag of vegetables from here. This is a market frequented by the Assamese urban gentry, bureaucrats and claimants of the city's heritage. The vendors are aware of it and enjoy the respectability that comes with the elite clientele.

As a child, Dwipen used to hitch a boat ride and come with his brothers to Maligaon market to sell a few pumpkins and often go back home with only a few annas. Now he has one of the largest shops here and even offers a glass of black tea with ginger to his regular customers. He doesn't forget to remind you like everyone else here that his products are all 'local.' The day he started growing and selling broccoli at the market was an exciting one for him.

On one side, a row of very small tea shacks serve as a canteen facility for the people working in here. There are specialized stalls for herbs and spices and condiments and even local varieties of rice. Ram Kanto collects these from the hills near Chay Gaon or sixth village, a township near Guwahati. The spices are cultivated by Khasis. Ram Kanto is probably a pseudonym which he uses for professional reasons.

At the far end are the fish and meat stalls. Chitol is a regular variety there. Chitol is a fish that deserves an exclusive description. It's flat with a mound towards the nape. Silvery white and has a large head but with a small mouth. It's bony but very yummy. I don't think the Bengalis have yet been able to establish a direct lineage to this fish, so it is still claimed by the Assamese. The Bengali have a number of chitol recipes which the urban Assamese may mistake as authentic Bengali cuisine. One of the most accepted chitol recipes would be the chitol macher mutha (the Bangals or people from East Bengal call it chitoler kola) or dumplings. It's divine. But I was informed by defenders of Assam's culinary tradition that chitol mutha is also Assamese. After all, the fish is the pride of the Brahmaputra. But the East Bengal loyalists claim that the same river flows into Bangladesh as Yamuna and has the same fish and hence, they too lay claim to the recipe.

However, the chitol in Magh Bihu is a matter of prestige without which the resident Assamese (and the resident Bengali) can suffer from mild bouts of depression.

A few paces away from the main Cachari market is the city's most open display of the varieties of fish. If it was a little more organized, it could make for a tourist attraction. Fishing boats that spend the night on the Brahmaputra arrive here early in the morning and sell their catch to the bigger players, who in turn sell it at the market price to petty vendors. The boatmen are generally Bengali Muslims, the business is run by the Assamese and the vendors are either Biharis or Bengali Muslims. In round containers made of tin attached to bicycles, these vendors spread out to all the city localities selling 'local fish', which often comes from the fisheries.

Now this is the most engaging discourse in Assam: 'local fish' versus 'chalani fish.' Local fish are the varieties caught in and around the state. Chalani means whatever comes from outside, mainly from Andhra Pradesh, Kanpur and Lucknow. The difference in cost is substantial. The taste is acquired. But yes, the taste of river fish is distinctly different from the fishery. A few years in Assam gives you an insight into the grades of fish. The Assamese is as loyal to a fish as a Bengali. The notion of identity here can be associated with the preparation of fish. Bengali fish preparation is identified with a lot of mustard, though I enjoy the jhol as well or the jhal, a green chilli gravy. Assamese fish discourse begins with tenga and goes through a variety of indigenous recipes like patot diya mach which is fish wrapped in banana leaves and steamed and the mach pura which is smoked fish. Fish is probably one of the most discussed creatures in the culinary world. But in Assam, cooking fish is all about being subtle.

When the self-styled chairman of ULFA was arrested and kept in a safe house in Guwahati, he was served patot diya mach and tenga as a homecoming gift. Mind you, he was under arrest.

NINETEEN

The Square Table

Imagine a square table covered with a white starched tablecloth. Two persons seated opposite each other. One is blindfolded. The other takes his seat and helps the other release the blindfold.

The white tablecloth has been witness to the confessions of the most brutal terrorists here. The colour is inconsequential. Sometimes it is olive green. Sometimes it is just bare wood. The room is musty and not secure at all. An armed security guard is supposed to attend to the confession but the interrogator gestures him to leave.

He was short, stout, bearded and had a calm presence. He had none of the physical aggression or appearance to convince you of his terrorist training. In the last six months, he must have killed more than a few hundred innocent people. But he was also sure he will not be hanged or even tried like other murderers. He was fighting for a 'cause.' If monuments across the country can glorify freedom fighters who have attempted to bomb or kill colonial intruders, then the logic of freedom struggle should apply to him as well.

The bearded man went to jail and was bailed out after a few months. Then he became the toast of seminars and workshops on conflict resolution. It seemed easy to resolve. Money and political power have never failed to purchase people however strong their convictions might have been.

Remoteness, conflict and a sense of persecution can produce some of the finest urban legends. Such was our Painterbabu. He painted pretty pictures and made lovely greeting cards. He was quiet and tolerant. He avoided the boys and preferred to keep to himself.

Then one day, he ran away. When he rediscovered himself, he was experimenting with weapons on human beings. The range and depth of his weapons created one of the longest trenches of mass graves in this country. The story goes that he would punish erring cadres by burying them alive, upside down.

Guwahati slowly changed. Then it started changing even more; but in the wrong direction. The political mafia ran its writ. The murderers shouted themselves hoarse. People slowly moved aside. The city with the most vociferous peoples' agitation of the 1970s suddenly died a natural death.

A Gypsy drove up on the main road of Guwahati with another vehicle following it. A sharp shooter watched his rear view guiding him to the vehicle behind and shot the driver on his temple. He then shot his right arm and carried on like a stunt sequence.

It's not always when a generation caught in the middle of their life can recount so vividly of their friends and acquaintances fighting a deadly war of vendetta. Every death is of a familiar face. Every killer – a former friend or an acquaintance. Nostalgia is tinged with pain. Anger spills over. Hatred walks on the streets. It's all about 'our' people. The fight against the 'other' people is now in our own backyard killing 'us.' Assam's 'nishpradip' had come full circle. Struggling to get out of the bloodied fields, it found an easier route to redemption.

TWENTY

Dylan on a Bedford Bus

At 4:46 pm when the young lovers were holding hands with trepidation and a light drizzle removed the dirt on the leaves, the sound of a thousand guitars strumming *Heal the World* together was magical. Music has been one instrument used by people in the north-east to heal their sense of alienation. But this image is also the biggest stereotype of these states and somehow, the grip has only tightened. Since the first Guinness Record on the largest ensemble of drums in Shillong, many states of the region wanted their own Guinness Record of music. Drums, bamboo dance, indigenous instruments and it promises to go on.

There is a trend in these states of 'habit formation.' It is a peculiar post-conflict behaviour where someone has just begun doing something and others will follow, till it hits a saturation point. For example, after the first big surrender of ULFA cadres, Guwahati was suddenly flooded with liquor stores. Millions of public telephone booths followed the liquor business. Momo counters came very close to compete with liquor and telephone booths. Chicken and egg roll shops are other favourites.

Momos deserve a special mention. Momo is almost a national food in these parts. Shillong was the capital of momos in the years before Sikkim was discovered. So the authentic Chinese and fake Chinese restaurants and fast-food corners served pork momos and it was believed that momos can only be made of pork. Then one day, a smarter businessman started selling chicken momos and even vegetable momos stuffed with cabbage.

The restaurants serving these dumplings were graded as amongst the best in the city. Two adjacent joints, Norling and Kalsang (no one cared where the names came from) are witnesses to probably the largest number of couples in their first hand-holding date in dingy cabins. Boys who could not afford a girlfriend, also visited these dimly-lit cabins with Asia 72 beer and plate of momos. It was mandatory to visit these joints where the whiff of ajinomoto tempted any passerby to stop over and consider spending a little time. Once you stepped inside, time is not a consideration.

For those who lived in Shillong beyond the first few years of adolescence, one graduated from those dingy kiss-me cabins to places like Snow White Restaurant which had similar cabins, a little spacious and opened rather early in the morning to accommodate lovers who wanted to stay away from classes and spend the day. A girl who owned the place would serve and that was a big selling point for the place. She was rude but men would bear that attitude to watch how she managed four mugs and two bottles pressed against her not-so-voluptuous breasts and maintain cold eye contact with her customers with a wry smile.

Momos came in different shapes and sizes and it was a binding force between the tribal and the non-tribal people. The non-tribals would otherwise hesitate to assimilate with the tribal food habit, but this was an imported cuisine – it was tasty, affordable and everyone's favourite.

But post-millennium youth of the north-east believed that the baggage of alienation was too regressive and detrimental, so a band of music lovers decided to play a different track. There was a conscious effort to shrug off the image of a guitar-strumming tribal youth. Suddenly music became a serious business.

They started singing the blues in Shillong. Hard Rock in Manipur. Pop in Nagaland.

Church choirs helped create a tradition of western music across the largely-Christian tribal areas of the region. At the same time, Hindu-Meitei Manipur was equally high on heavy metal and rock. Music was an inevitable expression but beyond a few rock shows and an odd album, most of the groups withered away, till Bob Marley entered Shillong. Keith, who went to school with me, took over as the music manager of the region, dreads and all. Keith and his brothers started singing with a purpose. 'No more cover numbers,' Keith said. 'Let's try doing our own stuff.'

Their father was singing in the Calcutta night clubs and never wanted any of his sons to pick up singing. All the sons took to serious music and exported north-eastern music along with their own, across the world. They helped usher in a sort of movement to raise money and generate revenue for the musicians. Several other groups including an all-girl band created a musical buzz.

There was a long-haired man who ran a tailoring shop and I always remember him running across the road near the post office in Laitumkhrah with a smile for all seasons. He would get on a running Bedford city bus that billowed smoke from a thin chimney near the front door. He would wave at invisible people as if he was waving to his fans. He sang Dylan and set his own compositions to music. He loved to show off his trademark shorts. The colour of his socks never matched and he was almost ritualistic about drinking liquor. Liquor made him smile.

It's only much later that this long-haired country musician became an institution and an icon. He was getting married for the fourth time and his shorts had climbed up a few centimetres more, exposing his rippling thighs. At an age when others were retiring from work, he was just peaking. He could sing through an entire evening without ever feeling weary, and many a time his wife joined him on stage.

Most of the young people didn't listen to any local bands as such. It was assumed that they were average. Even Lou was not as popular. A few groups started on their own with original compositions but did not make it anywhere. Musicians were still not making money. But nevertheless, the music was being made.

After two full decades of the killings and unrest, Shillong embraced a new reputation as a rock destination. Bands of musicians emerged and international groups made sure Shillong was a stop over on their Indian tours. The tambourine man was always around.

After long years of singing, Lou finally built his modest house. He went on collecting a window and then a door and then a chair with his meager earnings till he could call the four walls his home.

Along with a few other musicians, Lou had started The Great Society. It was not an underground, basement band of any sort. I cannot recollect a single lyric of the band. No band is worth it unless the words and tunes linger in your mind for a long time. But the band was among the first in the country. That was something!

Members of that band who live all over the country and few other faithfuls get together every year on Bob Dylan's birthday and sing. People join them. Dylan is the naturalized resident of Shillong and his music is the biggest inspiration for Lou and his friends.

One amongst them, Rudy, sustained his own band to sing the blues and soul and went much further from the stereotype. His was not a nostalgic trip. They were the first from India to have performed at the Memphis Blues Festival. His girlfriend Tipriti performs with him. I never knew about her though she lived in the same small town and she seems like someone who has just walked into the scene from a Kerouac novel, carrying with her a sensibility that is lyrical and free-spirited.

But musical Shillong found it difficult to grow out of its xenophobic tendencies. There was no music movement either. Neither did the colonial town have any intellectual or progressive activities. Two dozen poets would collect enough money to buy half-cups of bad tea and squat on a dusty carpet to read poems every Saturday. Only three of them grew up to be the city's designated poets. The rest have been published but will be forgotten. I too had just a few poems in print in the forgotten category. We were still writing of love and forgetting and were heavily under the influence of Latin American poets.

Shillong's predicament was different from her neighbours. It did not have a serious political situation but there was something dysfunctional about the people and the state. Its apparent tryst with peace was not reassuring even for someone like me who grew up there. Maybe I was too burdened with the violence to let music heal the wound. Music doesn't heal wounds. It momentarily makes you forget the pain.

But Meghalaya is much more about women power than its music. A little is misplaced and a lot is misinterpreted. Khasi women were more grounded. They looked after the house and earned a livelihood too but in a manner quite different from many other cultures. The popular perception was that while the men were growing their hair longer and swaggering around, attempting to make music, the women were running the home. Yet female emancipation was not guaranteed.

Khasi, Garo and Jaintia girls brought home their husbands and inherited the family property but despite the matrilineal system, the men dominated the politics of the state. The matrilineal system also had elements of patriarchy and women have actually never enjoyed the status others assume they have.

Most Khasi women have a betel nut fetish. Their ankles look like alabaster, rubbed and polished with pumice stone everyday but their teeth are red with betel nut. So they use the skin of nut to brush their teeth even in public. Most tribal women are uninhibited in their own ways. They never care about how others perceive them. Dignity of labour is very high and they are tireless workaholics.

Khasi women are not exactly enigmatic but they straddle both their tribal customs and the outside world with near perfection. I knew of a girl who managed top grades at the university but on her way home squatted alongside her mother to sell fish in an open air market.

I remember during monsoon how she would clean the fish and cut them into neat pieces before tying it on a cane string. If someone wanted the full fish, then the string would go through the mouth of the fish and customers would happily carry it in their hands and return home. Most people would prefer walking in Shillong those days. Now they have traffic jams down the main road.

TWENTY-ONE

School

Thanks for the photographs. Come on, confess, do I detect a faint hint of a tummy (like the rest of us, except B – he has got worms) or are you 'breathing in' your tummy? M, nice to hear from you after a long time, I wouldn't have recognized you if I met you in the street.

School voices melt into time but this was too damn recognizable. Ghosh had his signature style of writing the perfect sentence with wit and humour.

Chang, I will send you some pictures soon. Bow, your 6's and 9's rolled out so effortlessly. Nagi, nice to hear from you. The address and telephone numbers that you had given me in 2005 remain folded in my wallet. I heard Mathumal has started fasting for a separate state of 'Namboodripad.'

3 March 1974. A group of children were walking to a

beautiful school atop a small hillock. It was surrounded on all sides by other schools which must have been as good but this school stood out quite a bit. Now even more!

> *Two words about the state of affairs in our old school – hideous and sad. The main school building seems to be painted green, crimson and cream. Evidently, current management is not big on aesthetics. I also noticed a crude contraption/shelter immediately above 'blessed Edmund Rice' – the 'deification' of Edmund's is complete. Class 9B looks like it has been sawn in half, exposing the library windows. If I remember correctly, at lunch time guys used to call out 'I love you M' to the librarian through those windows and scoot before the stiffneck husband could catch them.*

M was the only young female in a school full of boys and celibate teachers. She would wear skirts and her long legs (which appeared longer than she must have had) allured rows of boys who would either follow her or ogle from windows and corridors. At any given time she would have a few dozen admirers imagining the most lucid dreams. But there were no rumours of her indulging in the admiration, although she must have enjoyed every bit of it. Her jealous husband had only one blazer which he wore every day without fail, and carried a stick-like umbrella. And he spoke like a robot.

At 10:20 a ten-minute break time meant devouring half the lunch to save time during lunch for a full hour of basketball. The rest of the lunch would be distributed or consumed during classes. But those playing fields have been neglected for too long.

The first field looks like a rhino enclosure and what's with the fencing all over the place? Do they want to keep the insiders from moving out or the outsiders from moving in? And why do they have to be so high? To think how we lovingly restored the cricket pitch and then covered it up with a mat – no questions asked. It was E's idea after all. Mitra, remember the cigarette burn you received from E? The handball courts are the saddest – it has neglect written all over it. This was the place where Gogoi used to employ the unusual technique of presenting the full face of his shoe while playing 'Kings.' Often he would miss the ball completely and get his family jewels rattled. What a shame.

Everybody carried tiffin boxes but lunch was unusually insipid. J's memories are almost vivid about the aluminum tiffin box he carried.

I really don't seem to have any recollection of what my mum packed for lunch. There would also be visits to the college canteen to eat tasteless buns with equally tasteless blobs of boiled potato (called aloo chops) sandwiched inside them. There is yet another reason why I don't seem to be able to recollect the contents of my lunch box. Every morning, during the 10:20-10:30 pee break, a character named Poddar used to beg of me – 'Pass some lunch, man!' He was a boarder and looked healthier than I, but he managed to convince the empathic part of me that he was severely malnourished by the hostel food. So, in Class IX, the lunch that my mother packed for her son usually found its resting place down another boy's throat. Now that you mention it, I realize that my lunch hour consumption during my school days was not a patch on what my children take to school. They literally order their lunch the previous night and lunch for them consists of chicken sandwiches, burgers, pastries, etc packed in one compartment and fresh fruits (the only fruits I knew were bananas and oranges) of all kinds packed inside another.

Some were luckier.

Lunch was roti-sabji, sandwiches, luchi-aloo sabji, noodles etc. Yes we did exchange lunch … like Chang says if the borders left anything to be shared. Borbora (God bless his soul) used to bring fried noodles quite often. There was this Mizo guy in class VIII (forget his name, started with an L) who used to bring momos … which were in great demand. When we had a spare 0.25p (which was the rate) we used to go to the tuck shop or to the channa walas/ice cream vendors near the main gate.

Then there were others.

Apart from the 'main course' (home food) the real delicacy were the boiled aloos sliced with some chutney and spice sprinkling and the ice cream at 25 paisa (the four anna doesn't exist any longer. The item mentioned was called golas). Available only outside the main school gate.

Twenty-eight years after passing out, it seemed to me that most schools develop ugly extensions of concrete, not in sync with its original design and structure. Like the many myths Shillong managed to carry forward to the outside world, one was about its coveted status in the field of education. We would hear people refer to Shillong as an educational town. I have always had serious reservations about it. It's with great difficulty that one can identify the scholars that Shillong has produced, at least in my generation. So what was it that gave Shillong a veneer of educational one-upmanship? Hill stations in India acquired this colonial validation of having good schools.

Maybe all hill stations with Christian missionaries have this scholastic thing about them. Nuns and padres around you instill a kind of confidence that they are committed to the task of imparting quality education to us. That's not necessarily the case. Only a miniscule of the padre population were good teachers. The others were part of the system, so they delivered without any inspiration.

Shillong's education was segregated. There was no attempt whatsoever at assimilation. The local language was alien to most people living there for years. Cross-cultural displays were unlikely items at school functions.

Last night, a thought crossed my mind. There are some fifteen friends who interact with each other quite regularly, none of whom is a Khasi. This is probably a reflection of the times that we lived and grew up in – the unmistakable dichotomy that has always been there in Meghalaya. The 'us and them' syndrome. It is kind of sad because deep inside I feel that I have lost out on a lot of the local culture by staying on one side of this cultural divide. I wonder if there is any other place where an 'immigrant' might be born and might grow up in without learning even the rudiments of the local language! Yet, all of us have achieved this unenviable feat. What is an even more telling statement of this apparent socio-cultural intransígence of mine is that in the four years that I spent in Kerala, studying for my engineering degree, I learnt more of Tamil (from Jaffna-Sri Lankan roommates) than I ever learnt Khasi in all my life. What is at fault – the inability of the locals to assimilate the outsiders into their system or the haughty stubbornness of the plainsmen to adopt any of the local attributes into their own lifestyles – this is a question that probably will have many answers in terms of versions, but none that will ever satisfactorily address the issue. Or, is it a unique case of two cultures coexisting in a single society, quite like the parallel lines of railway tracks?

That was not the entire truth. The truth was also camouflaged in the systemic apathy, political indifference and politicization of ethnic identity. Lines drawn were so sharp that friends turned around and the town which otherwise wore the habit of serenity suddenly exploded. Bombs didn't go off at once. Daggers were not drawn.

But the façade came off. The 'we' and 'them' determined every aspect of life.

There were areas in the tiny town which 'we' stayed away from and have never visited because 'they' would kill us if 'we' went. There were restaurants 'we' preferred going to because 'they' wouldn't harass us there. There were girls 'we' so wanted to chat up but refrained from because 'they' would attack us for doing so.

So a lot of 'we' left the hills and created their own image of childhood which would revisit them as pieces of nostalgia. The pine trees, the old Bedford city buses with Dylan playing through contraptions fitted in a World War II vehicle, the rain, the clouds and a rare vision of the alabaster skin girl who had pigtails and wore a short skirt with red and black stockings. Slowly 'they' became rich and powerful and 'we' acted like victims in a land that could never belong to us.

In that din of unspoken hatred, a group of young men and one or two women started writing poems of love and longing. The poems had nothing of the bloodshed and the pain and loss. Love was the overarching theme.

Postscript

Curfew. Sirens. Lathicharge. Tyres on fire. Trees felled and roads blocked. Neighbour's home set on fire. Bomb. IEDs. Grenades. Slogans. Dharnas. Rape. Killing. These are stereotypes. Images within which these places we travelled to are trapped . But these are also real images. Of course they coexist with the variety and gaiety of human life. Sometimes they affect the people but at other times they are just 'stories.' In this ceaseless and mindless violence, these stories are unpredictably resilient.

Murders are not counted here. They are mentioned occasionally.

Eshei entered this book much later. There were other people who filled up the names and places and then found their way out without notice. One day Eshei left too. Eshei was the name she chose for herself. Right from the very beginning, she had designed this entry and exit and when she lived in this book, she lived almost anonymously. There were leads but she covered her tracks very craftily. It started in the month of June. June is a cruel month.

By Sepetember Eshei was leapfrogging through the pages and its folktales and anecdotes. By November, she was breathing the words. Eshei meandered through the lines sometimes with defiance, as well as surrender. She is not a representative of any one community or culture. She is just one amongst us.

The book winds through personal anecdotes and emotional journeys to confront political realities and historical mistakes. Some of the characters are partially fictitious but its settings are to date. But history is always contested and so will the accounts of this book.

As you know by now, my first visit to Manipur was in 1989. I stayed with a poet friend Robin Singh Ngangom, whose letters and poems on exile have been reproduced here. Robin and I have spent numerous afternoons in Shillong collecting music and poetry. Journalist Pradip Phanjoubam and Yambem Laba took me around in Robin's family Ambassador car. My first impressions of the place and its people – I owe it to them. When I revisited Manipur as a journalist, it was Rupachandra Singh, a journalist himself and later an entrepreneur who introduced me to the several facets of the place. His cups of coffee which have now become tiny sips of tea were always available even during the worst of times.

Several young people have contributed to this documentation by sharing their life stories, their personal angst and sometimes even with their vehement disagreement with my perceptions.

I must express my gratitude to Chitra for accompanying

me to many places in Manipur and engaging me in several issues that she was confronted with.

I must acknowledge Ronid Chingangbam, a PhD student whose poem I used to describe a market in Imphal.

Not just help and encourgement but the interest of my friends saw me through this book. In Manipur, for example, Natasha Elangbam would ask regularly when the book would be out.

Basanta Rajkumar, a forest service officer from Punjab was like a ready reckoner and certified the chapters on Manipuri cuisine and history. He was full of details – a complete Meitei!

The Manipuri folktales would have never been told unless Sumitra allowed me to share her notes.

Kaimuanthang soldiered for years, taking me to the remotest areas and bringing back compelling stories, some of which have found their way in this narrative.

Theyie Keditsu, a foodie, musician and teacher wrote to me from Nagaland, but her story ended as abruptly as her visit.

Sunita has been very kind to share some of her stories on music and rituals which became my window into the mind of a generation.

Nicky Chandam, a Manipuri who writes in Urdu, took the trouble of correcting the factual errors and was the book's first reviewer. Khelena Gurumayum helped me understand the fragile balance of the tightrope her generation walked on, living in Manipur.

Gautam Sarma, an architect and several other personalities rolled into one, narrated stories from the Assam agitation to me.

Shillong, the place I grew up, is made up of my friends who have constantly been after me to write this book. Joydeep Choudhury has not let me rest since I decided to write. Jishnu, Subendhu, Deepak, Anirban and Manoj added their lunch time stories for the concluding chapter. I must add a missing person from this group of friends, Prasenjit, who would have certainly dominated the pages, had he been alive. My school St Edmund's – its idyllic setting, disciplinarian life with an Irish accent was my idea of growing up. Many people influenced my Shillong days but I must especially thank Professor Noorul Hasan for teaching me literature as well as irreverence.

I am grateful to Ranjana Sengupta for reading the first draft of the first chapter and asking me to complete the manuscript. Ayesha Kagal has patiently guided my professional work for a long time. I must mention Deepa Adhikari here: I borrowed a sentence that she had added to a script of mine.

I would like to thank NDTV. They allowed me to travel and report from these places. My camerapersons, Sanjay and Azam, who were truly my constant companions. It's through these travels that I met the most interesting storytellers, and fascinating people and cultures which only strengthens my conviction that the human heart ticks the same way everywhere in this world. To understand that, I had to accompany my friend DPK Pillay to Tamenglong, to report a soldier's return to a village where he was almost killed, a village he also helped keep alive.

There are numerous people, sounds, voices and images which have visited me repeatedly, that I have attempted to pass on through this disjointed narrative. Tisha Srivastava's letters from the forest dissolved into Eshei's own tiger tales. I must thank Akanksha Saxena who believed in the book and Eshei. Sumana Roy was ever encouraging and pulled the reins whenever I wavered.

I was amazed at how my mother Sobhona published two books on folktales while I was still struggling with a chapter. That helped me push myself. My father, a professor of history with his starched dhoti and kurta, had once said that all he left for me was his book. I have not been able to give him anything back as yet! My sister, my earliest (reluctant) play mate stood by me, believed in me. My uncles, Kulada, a filmmaker and a theatre personality and Kalyan, an artist, were my earliest teachers. My cousin Kishore, a poet and a folklorist, has been my best friend since the early years.

Rituraj Konwar, my photographer friend, who would always capture the moments I wanted to write about. His photo of two police commandos buying water lilies from a market of pavement florists was the first visual commentary of the book.

Anushree Majumdar, whose ability to sense the tone and tenor of the narrative has been invaluable.

I must thank Saugata Mukherjee, my publisher at Pan Macmillan India, who believed that the manuscript would actually end up as a book.

My daughter Shreya with her interest in storytelling, made me narrate many passages to her. I am humbled by her presence in my life.

Gayatri was the sole witness to how this was written amidst the vicissitudes of our togetherness and our separation. I thank her for everything.